THE
INTERNATIONAL
SCHOOL OF
SUGARCRAFT
SUGAR FLOWERS

I dedicate this book to my dear wife, Sindy, for her unfailing love and support, to my family and all my friends throughout the world.

I should like to thank the many people who helped me during my last world tour, including Bill, the House of Sugarcraft; A. O. K. Metals for supplying the stands shown; Gulnar, Bombay; the Taj Group, India; Le Meridien Hotel, Singapore; the Singapore Chefs' team; Gwen and Nola, Hong Kong; Mrs Imada, Toshie, Sue and all her staff, Tokyo; the Imperial Hotel, Tokyo; Jacky and Tony, Jill, Marie, Patricia, Shirley, Caroline and Morris, Australia; the Association and Guilds of Australia; everyone at Décor Cakes, Auckland; all members of ICES, Debbie, Oklahoma, and Joan, New York; and the personnel of all the different airlines I fly with.

I should also like to thank the team who worked on this book for their patience and understanding.

THE
INTERNATIONAL
SCHOOL OF
SUGARCRAFT
SUGAR FLOWERS

An inspirational book for
sugarcraft artists

Principal Teacher: Nicholas Lodge

MEREHURST

First published 1990 by Merehurst Limited
This edition published 1996 by Premier Books
Ferry House, 51/57 Lacy Road, Putney
London SW15 1PR

© Copyright 1996 Merehurst Limited

ISBN 1 897730 80 2

Previously published as Sugar Flowers From Around The World

Edited by Alison Leach
Designed by Jerry Goldie
Photography by Graham Tann, assisted by
Lucy Baker and Alister Thorpe
Styling by Barbara Stewart
Make-up and manicure by Jane Van Bruggen
Typeset by Rowland Phototypesetting Limited,
Bury St Edmunds, Suffolk
Colour separation by Fotographics Limited, U.K.–Hong Kong
Printed in China by Leefung-Asco

The Publishers would like to thank the following for their help
and advice:
Bekenal Products Company Ltd, 501F–502F Hockley Centre,
Vyse Street, Birmingham B18 6NE
The Chelsea Linen Company, PO Box 6, Tetbury,
Gloucestershire GL8 8EJ, for kindly supplying a selection of linen
and lace handkerchieves
Hamilworth Floral Products Ltd, 23 Lime Road, Dumbarton,
Dunbartonshire G82 2RP, Scotland, for kindly supplying wires
and silk stamens
The House of Sugarcraft, Unit 10, Broxhead Industrial Estate,
Lindford Road, Bordon, Hampshire GU35 0NY
Janet Elizabeth, 25 Four Acre Mead, Bishops Lydeard, Taunton,
Somerset TA4 3NW, for the perspex (plexi glass) cake separator
shown on the British wedding cake
C. M. Offray & Son Ltd, Fir Tree Place, Church Road, Ashford,
Middlesex TW15 2PH, for kindly supplying ribbons
Surfaces, Unit H, 51 Calthorpe Street, London WC1X 0HH, for
kindly supplying painted backgrounds, surfaces and textiles
Filtering Media Manufacturers (FMM), PO Box 8,
Rickmansworth, Hertfordshire WD3 4NW, for producing the
flower cutters

FOREWORD

My first introduction to sugarcraft in Britain was in 1984 when I saw the work of Nicholas Lodge. I was so deeply impressed with its delicate and elegant beauty that I started a sugar decoration course in my cake school on my return to Japan.

Four years later Nicholas Lodge visited my school in Tokyo and gave a special demonstration lecture. I was amazed by the way his exceptional talents had developed in the meantime. Every member of the audience was equally entranced by the exquisite artistry and imaginative quality of his sugarcraft.

His extensive travels all over the world, lecturing and demonstrating, have enriched him with broad vision and confidence. He has a great interest in the traditions of the countries he visits and is always eager to learn more about the different flora, so that he can share this knowledge with readers of his delightful books.

A love of flowers is universal. I had often thought how exciting it would be to reproduce different varieties in sugar to decorate celebration cakes. This book makes such a dream come true, with detailed instructions and photographs showing how to achieve beautifully realistic results.

Naturally I turned first to the section on Japan. The maple leaf is a popular artistic motif in my country. In the autumn the leaves are tinted – not a simple red but a dark and more· subtle shade of crimson, much favoured by the Japanese. I was astonished to see how Nicholas Lodge had reproduced the exact colour and shape of the leaf with such accuracy and definition. The flowers associated with the other countries described so clearly in this book are equally superbly illustrated. Many of the flowers are also shown on the spectacular wedding and other celebration cakes specially designed to convey Nicholas Lodge's impressions of the relevant region.

I should like to congratulate him on producing this truly fantastic book which will indeed be a permanent source of inspiration to every sugarcraft enthusiast. I wish him continuing success in making even more people aware of the creative opportunities in sugarcraft.

MINAKO IMADA
Founder of the Minako Imada Cake School, Harajuku, Tokyo
Member of the British Sugarcraft Guild

CONTENTS

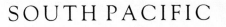

INTRODUCTION

When I was a student, I used to dream of being able to travel all over the world, meeting other sugarcraft enthusiasts and working in different environments. I now spend much of each year lecturing and demonstrating overseas and always return home with a notebook filled with ideas for new designs. The trip I made round the world in 1988 gave me some wonderful opportunities of seeing many exotic flowers growing in their natural habitats. This book is based on those experiences.

It is assumed that anyone wishing to make the flowers illustrated in this book will have a sound knowledge of all the basic sugarcraft techniques. Full details of these are given in *The International School of Sugarcraft, Books One* and *Two*, and *The Art of Sugarcraft – Sugar Flowers*.

It was quite hard to decide which flowers to choose for each region included in this book. Some of them, such as the frangipani, of course grow in several parts of the world.

Wedding cakes are not traditional in every country but I have tried to convey my impressions of the region in the choice of colours and the types of flowers displayed on the featured cakes. As they are primarily a means of displaying the flowers, the actual cakes are very simply decorated.

Some decorators find it difficult to think of suitable themes for men's birthday cakes, so most of the celebration cakes have been designed for such occasions. Many men are keen gardeners and this hobby provides plenty of scope for creating an appropriate design. In the section on North America, for example, a black-eyed Susan is shown winding up a bamboo cane. Other creepers, or even runner beans with their scarlet flowers, could be used in a similar way.

It is essential that all wires are inserted into a posy pick and never directly into the cake. If the flowers are to be arranged on the cake board or cake, the wired stems should be inserted into a small piece of sugarpaste. This is then applied to the cake, ensuring that the wires do not penetrate the cake surface. If any flower is wired, it is not of course edible.

Although special cutters are available for making many of the flowers shown in this book, it is always possible to use templates made from cardboard or empty plastic containers, such as those used for ice-creams.

Ideally, you should try to obtain a fresh bloom to use as a model. Some of the more exotic varieties may have to be specially ordered from a florist. With my love of flowers it is difficult to destroy one by carefully separating the different parts but this is the best way of reproducing it accurately.

You should allow plenty of time when making sugar flowers. Each part must be absolutely dry before dusting and finishing. The drying time of course varies depending on the level of humidity. If you are working in a very humid atmosphere, it is helpful to leave the flowers under a desk lamp until they are dry.

The realistic appearance of sugar flowers depends largely on the accuracy of the shading. You may need to experiment with different shades to achieve the desired result. It is always best to study the real flower closely for all the minute details that should be reproduced.

It is not necessary to use sable brushes; synthetic artist's brushes are perfectly suitable. Cosmetic brushes should not be used as they tend to be too soft. A flat paintbrush is needed to achieve intensity of colour over the total area, one petal or just an edge. You should use a round No3 or No4 brush for a soft overall colour. If you are working with different colours, clean the brush in cornflour (cornstarch) before applying another colour.

In some countries you can buy aerosol containers of vegetable fat, so that you can spray leaves, for example, to make them glossy. Elsewhere you should brush the surface lightly with white vegetable fat (shortening) at room temperature.

When using templates, make sure that the flower paste does not move on the board while you are cutting out the shape with a scalpel or modelling knife. When the paste is rolled out to the required thickness, smooth it with your fingers or the rolling pin on to the board to avoid any distortion while

cutting out the desired shape.

When joining two dry pieces together, use a little softened flower paste; egg white only works if one piece or both parts are still moist.

Damp and dust are the enemies of sugarwork. Flowers should be stored in a ventilated cardboard box, not a plastic or tin one. A sachet of silica gel will keep the contents moisture-free in a humid atmosphere.

If you have to transport decorated cakes, you should use as little packing as possible. If travelling in a car, place the cake on a thick foam rubber base that will cushion any bumps. If flying, it is important to check with the airline concerned the exact dimensions permitted for cabin baggage to ensure the box is the correct size.

One of the pleasures of making the flowers featured in this book was that I was reminded of the beautiful places where I had seen them growing, and all the charming people I had met on my travels.

INDIA

Stepping out of the air-conditioned plane on to Indian soil accentuated the intense heat and humidity of the April day at the beginning of my world tour. Although I had been to India and Sri Lanka on several previous occasions, this was the first time that I taught and demonstrated there. A close friend of mine, Gulnar, lives in Bombay; we had met in England when she attended one of my cake decorating classes. I was very fortunate to have her help in organizing demonstrations for me as she knew what would most appeal to the audiences, which were primarily composed of leading chefs and confectioners.

Traditionally, various sweetmeats are given to the guests at Indian weddings rather than wedding cake. Indeed the art of cake decorating is still in its infancy. This section opens with a two-tier wedding cake that I created to reflect the customs observed at Indian weddings.

Rich vibrant colours are needed in the decorations to complement the saris worn by the guests. The peacock is a sacred bird in India and Sri Lanka. The peacock feathers shown on the cake are made of rice paper. As the mogra and the marigold are used extensively in Indian festivals, I included these flowers in my design. The ivory colour of the icing was inspired by the elephant's tusk. Both the Taj Mahal and the elephant are often used as decorative motifs (see patterns on page 143), so I decided to reproduce these in flooded royal icing, a technique that proved of particular interest in India.

Both sponge and fruit cakes are made in India for celebrations. Unfortunately, the icing sugar that is obtainable there at present is coarse and quite grey-coloured. Gulnar had of course warned me about this so I had brought a supply with me.

MOGRA

Jasminum multiflorum

A dainty, pale ivory-coloured flower, the mogra has a very similar scent to jasmine, particularly strong in the humid night air. In the evening garlands of the flower are sold in the streets for men to give to their wives or girlfriends as a love token, just as red roses might be given in England. The garlands are either worn around the neck or, more usually, in the hair. With this romantic association the mogra seemed a very appropriate flower to use to decorate the wedding cake.

EQUIPMENT

paste colours and dusting powder

green-covered wire

paintbrush

template or special mogra cutter

porcupine quill

ball tool

fine white stamens

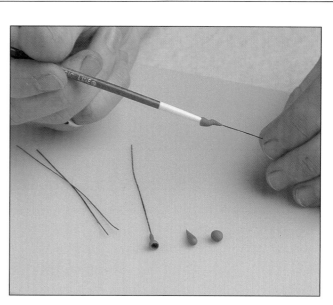

Roll a pea-sized ball of green-coloured flower paste into a cone. Dip a piece of hooked 30g green-covered wire in egg white and insert into the tapered end. With the end of a paintbrush hollow out the calyx, as shown. Leave to dry.

Roll out some ivory-coloured flower paste very thinly. Cut out seven petals for each flower, using either a template or a special mogra cutter. Do not try to make more than one flower at a time as the petals tend to dry out quickly. Vein each petal with a porcupine quill or cocktail stick (toothpick) and cup with a ball tool, as shown.

Brush a little egg white into the dry calyx. Think of this as a clock face. Stick one petal at 12, another at 6, then one at 4, another at 8, as shown. Stick the fifth petal at 12 and the last two at 10 and 5, making three layers. Place two fine white stamens in the centre. Leave to dry.

Dust a little moss green dusting powder into the stamens and around the centre of the flower.

Wire carefully into clusters of two or three flowers. Because of the position of the petals, they are very fragile so it is wise to make a few extra ones.

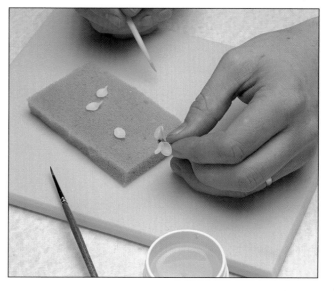

MARIGOLD

Tagetes erecta

In India the brightly coloured petals are scattered on the table at weddings and other celebrations, and the flowers are strung in garlands over doorways to celebrate birthdays and anniversaries. Orange is a colour that is much favoured for festive occasions which is the reason why I chose marigolds to decorate the wedding cake. The flowers are also very suitable for decorating a man's birthday cake. They can be used on their own or combined with other flowers.

| paste colours and dusting powders |
| green-covered wire |
| ball tool |
| cranked tweezers |
| small carnation cutter |
| paintbrushes |

Roll a small ball of green-coloured flower paste into a cone. Dip a piece of hooked 26g Nile green-covered wire in egg white and insert into the tapered end of the cone. Using a ball tool, hollow out the wider end to form a cup. Keeping the tool in place, pinch five ridges on to the calyx with cranked tweezers, as shown. Leave to dry.

Colour some flower paste with a mixture of yellow and orange paste colours. Roll out the paste and cut out six of the carnation shapes, using a small carnation cutter. Frill each edge with a cocktail stick (toothpick), as shown. Cover the remaining shapes with plastic wrap to stop them drying out.

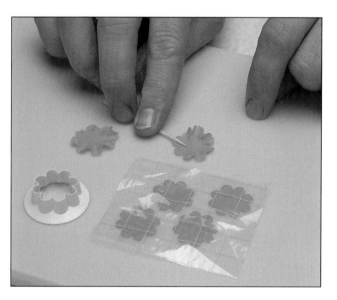

Use egg white to stick three of the shapes together, then cup with a ball tool. Brush the calyx cavity with egg white and press the shapes into it, to ensure they stick. Do the same with another two shapes. Cut a quarter section out of the sixth shape and roll the remaining piece into a cone, as shown. Brush with egg white and stick into the calyx. Leave to dry.

Dust a little green dusting powder into the centre. Brush over the whole flower with orange dusting powder. Then, using a flat paintbrush, brush yellow dusting powder over the edge of the petals to give these some shading. Finally, brush some plum dusting powder on to the protruding areas of the calyx.

LOTUS BLOSSOM

Lotus

A member of the water-lily family, the lotus blossom is a symbol of Buddhism and is considered sacred by the followers of this religion. Buddha is usually depicted seated in a lotus blossom. Every part of the plant is used: its roots as a vegetable and as starch; its sap for medicinal purposes; its fibres for lamp wicks; its seed heads dried for flower arrangements. The real flower measures about 25cm (10in) in diameter but the sugar version shown here has been scaled down to a more suitable size for decorating a cake.

ivory or cream cotton (thread)	
green-covered wires	
paste colours and dusting powders	
sweetcorn (mealie) leaf veiner	
small ball tool	
silk or plastic water-lily leaf	
No4 round paintbrush	

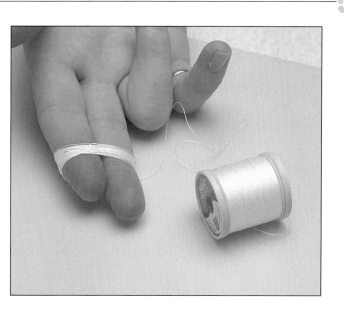

Wind some ivory or cream cotton (thread) round your first two fingers about 70 times, as shown. Be careful not to wrap it too tightly! Squash the cotton between your fingers and wrap a piece of 30g green-covered wire tightly around one of the folded ends. Cut the cotton, as shown.

About two-thirds of the length of the cotton, place your finger down the centre to flatten the cotton and make it look like a chimney sweep's brush. Brush a little pale pink and lemon dusting powder on to the cotton to give it a shaded effect.

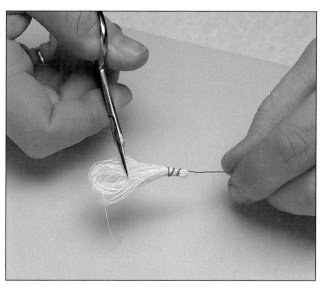

Make a small ball of cream-coloured flower paste into a flattened cone. Dip a piece of hooked 26g green-covered wire in egg white and insert in the paste. Make holes in the flat part, as shown, with a small ball tool or the end of a paintbrush. Thread the wire through the centre of the stamen piece until it rests on top of the cotton. Tape down the wire to secure the two parts together tightly.

Tape three pieces of 26g green-covered wire together and bend, as shown overleaf. Mould a piece of pink-coloured flower paste into a cone for the bud and stick on to the hooked end of the wire that has been dipped in egg white (see overleaf). Make sure that you mould the wider part of the bud around the wire securely.

continued overleaf

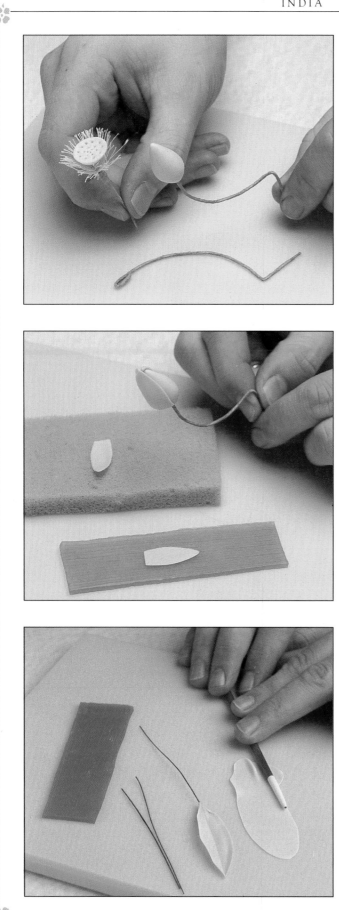

LOTUS BLOSSOM
continued

Roll out some pink-coloured flower paste and cut out four small petals, as shown. Place each one on a sweetcorn (mealie) leaf veiner or actual leaf and cup slightly with a ball or dog bone tool. Place in position, as shown, on the bud, slightly overlapping each other.

For the larger petals, roll out a piece of pink-coloured flower paste, retaining a thicker area. Roll this into a tubular shape from the centre outwards with a paintbrush, as shown. Cut out the petal and insert a piece of hooked 30g wire that has been dipped in egg white in the tubular shape. Roll a paintbrush or cocktail stick (toothpick) over the edges of the petals to soften them. Place over a concave surface to dry to give a cupped shape to the flower when assembled. You will need about 12 petals for each flower – for instance, eight large and four medium.

If you need any leaves, roll out some dark green-coloured flower paste. Cut out the shapes and press on to a silk or plastic water-lily leaf to mark the veins. Then soften the edges to give a little movement. Leave to dry. Brush with vegetable fat to give a natural gloss.

Use a No4 round paintbrush to dust the tips of the petals and the bud with pale rose pink dusting powder, as shown in the photograph of the finished flower.

Starting with the smallest petals, work clockwise putting each one in position. Tape firmly to ensure they are positioned correctly around the base. Finish the bud by placing a green calyx around the base of the flower.

Assemble in a posy pick on the cake so that the bud stands up, with the leaf flat and the flower slightly raised.

LOTUS BLOSSOM CAKE

The flower makes a dramatic focal point for the simply decorated celebration cake that I created for my friend Gulnar.

TUBEROSE

Polianthes tuberosa

The tuberose is a white Indian flower which is very similar to stephanotis. Like marigolds, tuberoses are used in many festivities in India; they too are formed into swags and draped over doors. In other countries including Hawaii tuberoses are used in *leis* which are hung around the neck. In India the fragrant waxy-looking flowers are used to adorn temples and are also carried with other flowers by the bride. The wedding ceremony is elaborate, the details varying in accordance with local customs and family traditions. The petals of a tuberose vary in number.

small calyx cutter
fine embroidery scissors
wooden dowel
green-covered wire
pale green stamens
paintbrush
dusting powders

Form a tiny ball of white flower paste into a cone, then mould this into a mushroom shape. Using a fine skewer or paintbrush, roll outwards from the cone gently to thin the base, as shown. This principle is usually known as the Mexican hat method.

Using a small calyx cutter, cut out the paste to make the basic flower shape, as shown. With fine embroidery scissors or your finger nails, cut or pinch off the fine pointed ends of the calyx. Squeeze each petal between your thumb and first finger to give a more natural shape to the finished flower.

Using a porcupine quill or cocktail stick (toothpick), make a fine groove around the inside edge of each petal, supporting this on a piece of foam rubber as you do so. Then make a rounded cavity in the centre with the tip of a wooden dowel, holding the flower lightly between your thumb and first finger, as shown.

Dip a piece of hooked 26g green-covered wire in a little egg white. Thread the wire through the centre of the flower. Mould the base around the wire to secure.

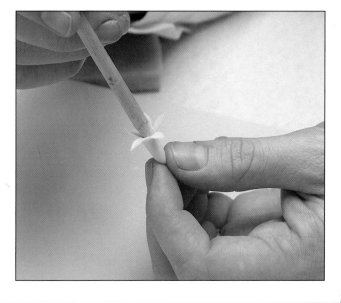

Assemble six tiny pale green stamens and position in the centre of the flower. Using a fine dry paintbrush, dust a little yellow dusting powder into the centre. Finally dust green dusting powder lightly around the base of the flower.

SOUTH-EAST ASIA

Several hundred miles separate Hong Kong and Singapore, two fascinating cities in South-East Asia that I always enjoy visiting. In both places the majority of the population is Chinese. Fortunately many people speak English very fluently so I have been able to learn about local customs.

There are innumerable colourful festivals and parades, both secular and religious, throughout the year. The Chinese New Year is the most important occasion and is celebrated on different dates between the end of January and the middle of February. Enormous flower markets are specially erected in Victoria Park on Hong Kong island and in other places, where whole families choose flowers to decorate their homes for this auspicious occasion.

Although it is not traditional to have a wedding cake, this custom is becoming more accepted, especially if the bride has been to Europe or the United States to study. The naturally artistic qualities of the Chinese have long been evident in their presentation of food. Not only do they cut vegetables into decorative shapes as a garnish, but they also carve fat and ice for special occasions.

Red and gold are a typical Chinese combination, so I chose these colours for this two-tier wedding cake decorated with a spray of anthuriums. The black borders make a striking contrast to such vibrant colours. The dragon is an important symbol in Chinese culture. The sides of the cake are decorated with gold fans. Patterns for making templates for both the dragon and the fans are given on page 143.

ANTHURIUM

Anthurium Andreanum

Anthuriums look so unreal that it is not surprising that people often think they are made of plastic or wax. In the tropical conditions of South-East Asia they grow outside, whereas in more temperate climates they need the protection of a hothouse. As they will last for up to three weeks in water, they are very popular with flower arrangers. The true flowers are found on the spike and what is shown here are the bracts or modified leaves. These range in colour from white and green to the deep red chosen for the sugar version.

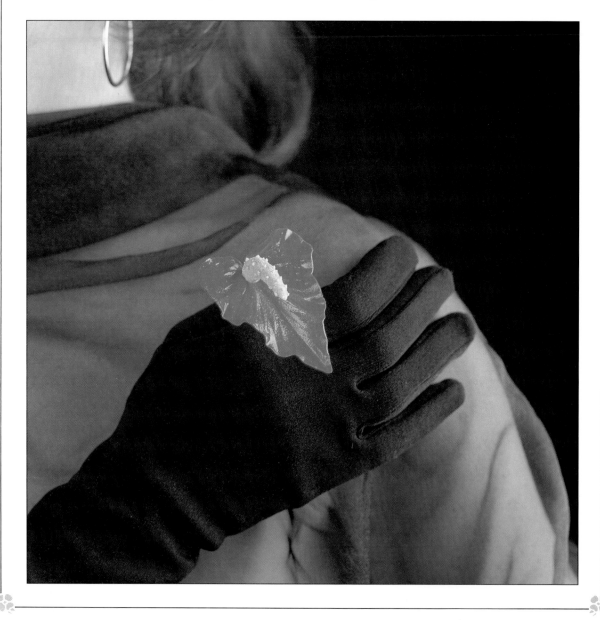

EQUIPMENT

paste colours and dusting powders
green-covered wire
semolina, ground rice or maize meal
heavily embossed veiner
No0 piping nozzle (tip)
royal icing

Roll a ball of yellow-coloured flower paste into a long tapered cone for the spadix. Dip a piece of hooked 26g green-covered wire in egg white and insert into the thicker end. Bend the cone over to the required shape. Tape two additional wires to the main one to make a thicker stem.

Colour some semolina, ground rice or maize meal with yellow dusting powder. Brush a little egg white over the spadix and dip in the semolina to give it a coating, as shown. Leave to dry.

Roll out some red-coloured flower paste for the bract. Cut out the heart shape and vein on one side only on a heavily embossed veiner. Mark a vein down the centre and soften the edge, as shown, with a cocktail stick (toothpick). Wrap around the spadix, sticking the two parts where they meet with egg white.

With a No0 piping nozzle (tip) and some pale yellow-coloured royal icing, pipe small dots of icing all over the spadix, as shown. Some anthuriums have only a few of these dots, others have hundreds. Any dots that have spikes can be touched with a moist paintbrush to make them more rounded. Leave to dry.

Dust a little green dusting powder on the spadix and brush a very thin film of vegetable fat over the bract to give the characteristic waxy appearance.

BAMBOO

Bambusa arundinaria

Bamboo grows in thick groves throughout South-East Asia and no part of the plant is wasted. The shoots are cooked; the wood is used to make furniture, baskets and even boats. It is also the staple diet of the giant panda in China. As bamboo is very easy to make in sugar, it is an ideal subject for even a complete beginner. The same principles apply to making similar decorations like twigs with blossom. Bamboo blends well with most colours, such as the pale pink chosen for the birthday cake on page 31. Another example of using bamboo is shown on page 110.

EQUIPMENT

EQUIPMENT

paste colours

porcupine quill or veining tool

cranked and plain tweezers

green-covered wire

sweetcorn (mealie) leaf veiner

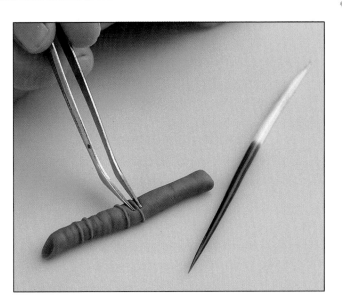

Roll a thin sausage shape of brown-coloured flower paste. Use either a porcupine quill or veining tool to make ridges along the paste. Two pairs of tweezers, one cranked and one plain, are needed to pinch the ridges effectively, as shown.

If you want to make longer pieces, you can insert a wire down the centre for support. As the paste must be soft when the leaves are added, keep in a plastic bag or under cover.

Flatten a small piece of green-coloured flower paste and roll out two-thirds. Then roll the remaining third so as to leave a thin tubular shape in the centre. Insert a piece of hooked 30g green-covered wire, that has been dipped in egg white, into the thick end. Cut out the shape of the leaf. Vein both sides on a sweetcorn (mealie) leaf veiner, as shown, or dry leaf. Leave to dry.

Cut off most of the wire, leaving just a small piece on each leaf. Stick the dry leaves into the soft brown sausage shape. Alternatively, you can make the leaves first and leave to dry. Then make the brown part and stick the leaves into position immediately.

Mix brown colouring with clear spirit and brush all over the brown part. Brush the leaves with vegetable fat to give them a slight gloss, as shown. Leave until dry.

The bamboo can be wired in sprays, or it can be arranged with flowers such as the vanda orchid, as shown on page 31.

VANDA ORCHID

Vanda

The vanda – Singapore's national flower – is one of my favourites in this large genus of the orchid family as the range of colours including shades of pink, mauve and apricot is so beautiful. This particular variety is very common in Singapore, Thailand and Malaysia. When I was in Singapore, I had the opportunity of visiting an orchid farm which made me realize the enormous potential of making some of these exotic flowers in sugar. Vandas grow on spikes like cymbidium orchids and can be wired into a spray.

EQUIPMENT

paste colours and dusting powders
veining tool
ball tool
green-covered wire
florist's tape
paintbrushes

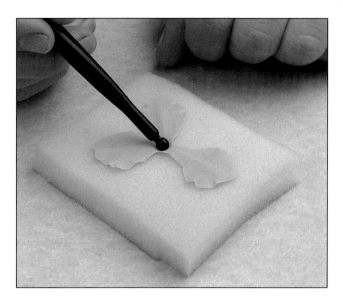

Roll out some pink-coloured flower paste and cut out the sepals in one piece. Frill the edge softly and vein down the centre of the petal. Turn the paste over so as to have inverted veining. Cup the centre of the sepals with a ball tool, as shown.

Make a hole in the centre with a cocktail stick (toothpick), as shown. Fold a piece of cardboard and prop up the top sepal, as shown. Leave to dry.

Roll out some pink-coloured flower paste, retaining a thin tubular base. Cut out one petal, then turn the template over so that you have a correct pair of petals, not two identical petals. Dip a piece of hooked 30g green-covered wire in egg white and insert into the thicker part of the petal. Soften the edge, as shown, and vein the back.

The throat is made in a very similar way to the oncidium orchid (page 38). Roll out some pink-coloured flower paste, leaving it thicker at one end. Cut out the throat so the part at the base is cut from the thicker part.

continued overleaf

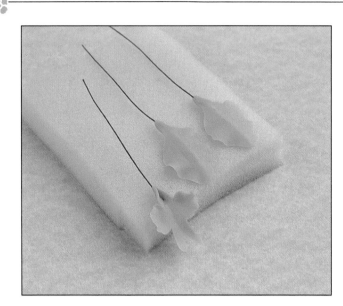

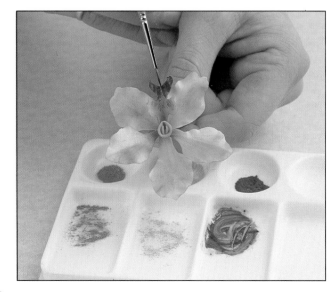

VANDA ORCHID
continued

Frill the two wing parts and mark a vein down the centre. Cup the two wing parts. Brush a little egg white on to the base. Lay a piece of hooked 30g green-covered wire on this, fold the paste over and roll into a tube, as shown. Leave to dry.

Thread the wing petals and throat through the hole in the sepal. Secure all the parts together by sliding a thin cone of paste down the back and then taping the wires. Bend the petals and throat into the correct position with tweezers.

Dust with pink dusting powder as shown, using a flat paintbrush around the main central vein. Dust the throat a peachy colour. Then mix some plum dusting powder with clear spirit and paint on the lines, as shown, with a fine paintbrush.

Hollow out a little ball of paste like a cup and position in the centre, with a small split apricot-coloured ball inside to represent the column and the stigma of the flower, as shown.

VANDA ORCHID CAKE

The decorative theme is repeated on the scalloped fan on which the inscription has been piped in Chinese characters.

JASMINE

Jasminum officinale

Jasmine is another flower that has a wonderful scent, especially in the humid night air of South-East Asia, or after rainfall. Some varieties are completely white, while others, like the one shown here, have a delicate plum colour on the back of the flower. Jasmine is comparatively quick to make so is a good secondary or filler flower to use in sprays for display purposes. It can also be used on its own or combined with other flowers to decorate a cake.

EQUIPMENT
paste colours and dusting powders
small calyx or jasmine cutter
green-covered wires
white stamens
porcupine quill
modelling knife

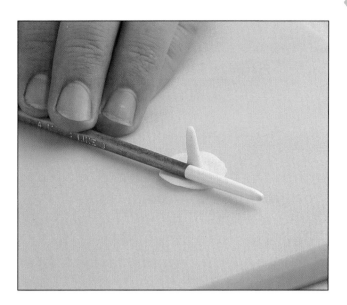

Form a small ball of white flower paste into a cone. Squash the end between your thumb and first finger to make a toadstool shape. Roll from the centre outwards with a paintbrush, as shown.

Cut out the petals with either a small calyx or jasmine cutter. If you are using a calyx cutter, you must pinch each of the ends to remove the very sharp points. Roll over each of the petals with a cocktail stick (toothpick) or paintbrush in the position shown so that the centre of the flower will not be spoilt by the point of the cocktail stick digging into it.

Make a hole in the centre with a cocktail stick. Thread a piece of 30 or 33g wire that has been hooked and dipped in egg white through the hole until the hook just disappears into the throat of the flower. Mould the paste around to give a long thin back, as shown. Place a single white stamen in the throat. Leave to dry.

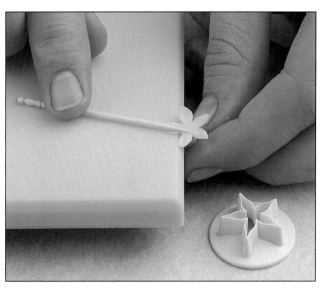

Make the buds by moulding long thin cones of white flower paste. Insert a hooked wire into each tapered end and push up the length of the bud to give it total support. Mark the ends with a porcupine quill to give the effect of the bud opening. Leave to dry.

Dust some pink/plum dusting powder all over the back of the flower and up about three-quarters of the bud. Then dust some soft lemon dusting powder into the centre of the flower.

Make the leaves from dark green-coloured flower paste and attach to 33g wire. Cut out free-hand using a modelling knife. Mark a vein down the centre. When dry, they can be brushed with vegetable fat to give a natural gloss.

TIGER LILY

Lilium tigrinum

The colouring of these striking flowers makes them a particularly appropriate choice to decorate a cake for an autumn wedding or a man's birthday. When you have mastered the technique of making a tiger lily, you will be able to adapt the shape and colour to reproduce other members of the exquisite lily family. It looks elegant in the form of a spray, either on its own or perhaps combined with oncidium orchids, as shown on the celebration cake on page 36.

EQUIPMENT

paste colours and dusting powders

lily stamens

fine pointed tweezers

green-covered wire

porcupine quill

paintbrushes

wooden dowel

florist's tape

Bend six lily stamens at right angles with fine pointed tweezers so that the groove is at the top, as shown.

For the pistil, roll a ball of orange-coloured flower paste into a tube. Insert a piece of 26g wire that has been hooked and dipped in egg white and push right up the wire to match the length of the stamens. Mark and divide it into thirds at the top, pinching each part like making a petal for a pulled flower.

Stick a tiny ball of green-coloured flower paste on the bottom of the pistil, as shown, to make the lobes. Mould into an oval shape and make six ridges with the pointed end of a porcupine quill.

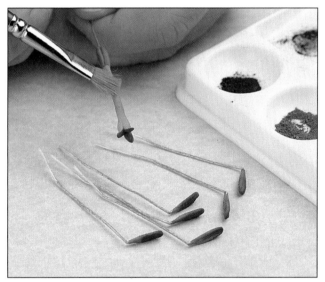

Dust the stamen cotton with orange dusting powder and the tops with brown, using a flat paintbrush, as shown, to get the intense colours – a round paintbrush would not give the same intensity of colour. The pistil is dusted brown and the column part green, as shown.

Roll out enough orange-coloured flower paste for each petal, keeping a thin tubular piece, as shown. Cut out petal shape. Insert a piece of wire and mould around the base to ensure it is secure.

Mark a vein down the centre of the back of each petal and soften the edge with a cocktail stick (toothpick) or paintbrush to make it slightly frilled, as shown overleaf. Lay the petal, veined side down, over a dowel to dry in the correct shape, as shown. You will need six petals; make three slightly more ruffled than the others. Leave to dry.

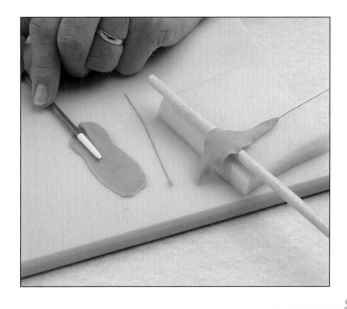

continued overleaf

TIGER LILY
continued

Tape the stamens in a ring round the pistil, as shown. Dust the petals with orange dusting powder and green at the base. Mix violet, plum and black dusting powders together to make a dark burgundy colour; mix this with clear spirit and paint the spots on each petal with a fine paintbrush.

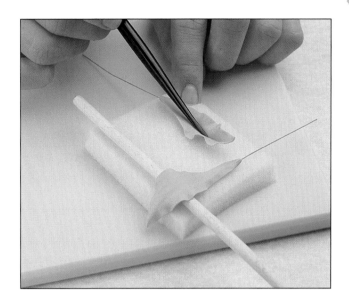

Bend the three smaller petals slightly using tweezers to prevent them snapping, as the wire is thicker than usual. Arrange these petals in a triangular shape and tape together round the central stamen and pistils. Then tape the remaining petals securely in between, as shown.

Mould a piece of green-coloured paste into a cone shape, thread the thicker part up the wire first and mould around the base of the flower. This forms the calyx and also fills in the gaps between the petals, giving a more realistic effect.

For the bud, tape three pieces of 26g wire together, hook one end and dip in egg white before inserting into the thicker end of a large cone of orange-coloured flower paste. Mark six deep veins with a porcupine quill or veining tool.

Make the leaves in the same way as the petals, using 28g wire and mid-green-coloured flower paste.

AUTUMN CELEBRATION CAKE

The shaded leaves of the spider plant blend well with the tiger lily and oncidium orchids, arranged as a spray, on the left-hand page of this book-shaped celebration cake.

ONCIDIUM ORCHID

Oncidium

Not only is there a memorable collection of orchids growing prolifically in the Botanical Gardens, but many species can be bought very inexpensively in the florists and flower markets of Singapore. Unlike some tropical flowers they last well in arrangements. The oncidium is very dainty which makes it ideal to use as a filler with larger orchids or lilies. There are many varieties of oncidium orchids in several different colours. The variety and colour of those shown here is matched to some that I admired in Singapore.

EQUIPMENT

paste colours and dusting powders
orchid cutter
veining tool
green-covered wire
paintbrush

Roll out some yellow-coloured flower paste, making it slightly thicker at one end. Cut out the throat, with the top piece that will make the tubular shape, from the thicker end.

Dip a piece of hooked 26g green-covered wire in egg white and lay on the top of the throat. Wrap the paste around the hook and roll between your thumb and finger to form a tube. Frill with a cocktail stick (toothpick) and mark a vein down the centre of the throat, as shown.

Roll out some more yellow-coloured flower paste and cut out the back part of the orchid. Frill the two wider petals slightly and vein the centre of all parts. Think of the shape like a matchstick man and cup his head and legs (the sepals). Thread on to the wire and stick on to the back of the throat with a little egg white. Place a minute ball of yellow-coloured flower paste at the base of the throat for the stigma and mark in half with a cocktail stick. Leave to dry.

Brush all over with yellow dusting powder, with a little green around the stigma and base of the flower. Mix some red and yellow paste colours with clear spirit to make a terracotta colour. Paint the details with a No0 or No00 paintbrush.

Make buds in various sizes, placing frilled rose petals over the larger ones to give the effect of their opening. Dust in the same shades as the flowers.

Wire an assortment of flowers and buds into a spray, referring to the main photograph for positioning. Mix some white dusting powder with clear spirit to the consistency of thin cream. Add some green paste colour to make it a mid-green. Holding the end of the stem, paint the stems and tape to make it more realistic.

BIRD-OF-PARADISE

Strelitzia reginae

Known as the bird-of-paradise because of its birdlike appearance, this flower originated in Southern Africa but now grows in abundance in many tropical countries. Its botanical name was given in honour of Queen Charlotte of Mecklenberg-Strelitz, the wife of George III. In South-East Asia it is used in large fresh flower arrangements by itself or with other tropical flowers. Made in flower paste, the bird-of-paradise looks very dramatic on wedding or other celebration cakes; one or three flowers could also be used in an *ikebana*-type arrangement.

EQUIPMENT

paste colours and dusting powders
strelitzia cutter
green-covered wires
veining tool
sweetcorn (mealie) leaf veiner
florist's tape

Colour some flower paste with a mixture of mauve and blue paste colours. Roll out a piece, making it slightly thicker at one end. Place the square end of a strelitzia cutter over the thicker part and cut out a shape. Roll the thicker end slightly to hollow it, as shown.

Dip a piece of hooked 26g green-covered wire in egg white and lay in the hollowed part. Roll into a tube and mark a vein down the centre, as shown. Cut out two petal shapes and wrap round the wire to form a tube.

Flatten a ball of orange-coloured flower paste and roll out two-thirds thinly into an oblong. Then roll out the remaining third thinly from the centre outwards on both sides, keeping a small sausage shape in the centre. Cut out a petal shape from the thicker part.

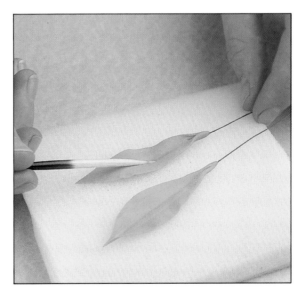

Dip a piece of hooked 28g wire in egg white and press into the thicker end of the petal. Vein with a sweetcorn (mealie) leaf veiner. Mark one main vein down the centre and two veins on either side. Make five petals for each flower. Leave to dry.

Bind three lengths of 24g wire together with green florist's tape and bend at a right angle about 6cm (2½in) from one end. Tape the petals along this length in the following order: one mauve, one orange, two orange, one mauve and two orange. Cover the base of the flower head with green-coloured flower paste.

Roll out some more green-coloured flower paste about 1.5mm (¹⁄₁₆in) thick and cut out the large base shape. Wrap this around to make the casement pod. Then cut out two or three of the elongated petal shapes to make the bracts, as shown in the main photograph.

Brush or spray all over with vegetable fat and brush the appropriate dusting powder into the fat on the green part to achieve a blended effect, as shown.

DENDROBIUM ORCHID

Dendrobium

More commonly known as the Singapore orchid, dendrobiums are medium-sized. They are very popular with florists for an ivory co-ordinated wedding. When I was making the flower shown here, I was reminded of a beautiful bouquet that I was given in Singapore after a demonstration. I made a template for the petals by dissecting a real flower and drawing round the petals. With my love of flowers, this caused me some anguish but it is the best way to reproduce such a bloom accurately. To make a spray, study a real one for the positioning of the flowers.

Cut out a shape slightly larger than the sepals from an empty drink can. Curve each part to the correct shape and make a hole in the centre with a bradawl.

Roll out some pale ivory-coloured flower paste and cut out the sepals. Place on a fine veiner so the back of each sepal has veining with reverse veining on its front. Soften the edges with a cocktail stick (toothpick). Place over a former and make a hole in the centre, as shown.

Roll out some more paste and cut out the two wing petals. These have a central vein on the front, not on the back. Soften the edges and stick in position with egg white. Prop the petals with a little foam rubber until they are dry, as shown.

Make the column for the throat by sticking a small cone of paste on to the end of a piece of 26g wire that has been hooked and dipped in egg white. Vein on both sides with a veining tool so it is like a heart shape at the top.

Roll out some more paste and cut out the throat shape. Cut the two sides to curve them, vein the centre and frill the base slightly. Brush the base of the column with a little egg white and stick the throat around it. Leave to dry over an orchid throat former.

Then thread the column piece through the sepal part. Slide a small cone of paste up the back of the orchid along the wire and stick with egg white. Leave to dry.

Dust a very pale green dusting powder around the centre part of the orchid. Make a small tapered sausage of flower paste for the pollen tract. Stick into the throat and mark in half with a porcupine quill, as shown in finished photograph.

JAPAN

Japan or 'the land of the rising sun' comprises a chain of mostly mountainous islands extending over a distance of about 1700 miles, yet more than a tenth of the population lives in the Tokyo conurbation. The rich heritage of traditional customs makes a fascinating contrast to the hi-tech achievements of contemporary Japanese industry.

My last visit to Japan coincided with the end of the spectacular blossom season when petals fell like pink confetti in the Emperor's Gardens in the gentle spring breeze, reminding me of the opera *Madam Butterfly*. Cherry blossom is such a feature of Japan that it has even been depicted on a coin.

Cake decorating has only become popular in the last few years; it seems a natural progression from other long-established arts such as embroidery and *ikebana*. In Japan people usually hire a polystyrene dummy rather than have an actual wedding cake. Many of these creations are very large and are often based on ultra-modern geometric styles.

However, I decided to design a cake with a theme of blossom time, using the pastel colours which are chosen for most Japanese weddings. Peonies are the main focal flower in each spray of blossom. A few petals, like those I saw in the Emperor's Gardens, are sprinkled over the cake.

In Japan the first plum blossom is preserved in salt crystals. Two or three flowers are placed in a fine porcelain cup at a wedding and hot water is poured over them. The drink tastes slightly salty but it smells fragrant.

Most traditional Japanese brides have two or three wedding dresses – usually one or two *kimonos* and a Western-style wedding dress; these are all worn at different stages of the wedding ceremonies and subsequent festivities.

BLOSSOM

Prunus

The perfect time to visit Japan is in the spring when the profusion of different types of cherry, plum and almond blossom is exquisitely beautiful. It reminded me of a pink version of jacaranda time in Harare, Zimbabwe. Blossom is invaluable in sugarcraft as it can be wired into sprays of so many different shapes and sizes. Larger sprays look very effective combined with other flowers on celebration cakes. Miniature sprays could be used to hold place cards at a formal dinner party.

EQUIPMENT

paste colours and dusting powders

yellow stamens

green-covered wires

green and brown florist's tapes

large blossom cutter

wooden dowel

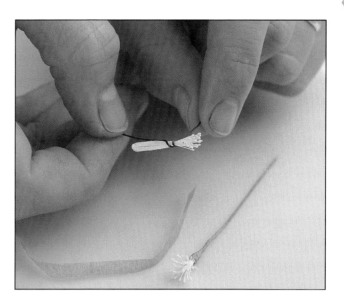

Fold 10–12 yellow stamens in half and wrap a piece of 33g green-covered wire around the folded part, as shown. Cut off the excess part of the stamen cotton. Cover the wire with a strip of ⅓-width green florist's tape, then cover this with ¼-width brown florist's tape to give a smooth finish.

Make a Mexican hat shape in some pink-coloured flower paste. Cut out each blossom with a large blossom cutter. Make a hole in the centre with a wooden dowel, as shown. Frill the edge of the petals gently with a cocktail stick (toothpick).

Brush a little egg white just under the stamens and push the wire through the throat of the blossom, as shown.

To make the buds, cover a piece of 33g wire with brown tape. Hook and dip the end in egg white and insert in a small ball of pink-coloured flower paste. Mark five lines on the bud, using a porcupine quill or cocktail stick.

Dust the buds and flowers with pink dusting powder. Some flowers are dusted all over, others only on one or two petals, to give a natural effect. Mix some moss green paste colour with clear spirit and paint five tiny leaf shapes at the base of each bud and flower to resemble a calyx. Leave to dry for about 5 minutes before attaching to 26g wires with brown tape, following the main photograph for positioning.

PEONY

Peonia

The terms for describing flowers in Japan are quite different
from those used in the West. For example, the peony is called 'wealth
and honour' or 'the king of flowers'. It is often featured in *ikebana*
arrangements with pine branches in the early spring. The peony shown
here is about one-third the size of the real flower but could of course be
made smaller or larger if wished. There are many varieties and colours of
peony. Peonies are featured on the three-tier wedding cake on page 45,
combined with sprays of blossom.

EQUIPMENT

paste colours and dusting powders
flat flower former
medium-sized calyx cutter
plastic tulip petal
fine yellow stamens
florist's tape
round paintbrush

Grease a flat flower former with a little vegetable fat. Roll a piece of white flower paste into a thin sausage shape and make into a ring around the top of your little finger. Then place on the former.

Roll out some green-coloured flower paste. Cut out a medium-sized calyx and lay on the ring, as shown. Do not stick it down as the ring is only to support the flower until it is dry.

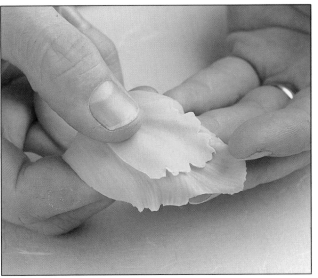

Roll out some pink-coloured flower paste very thinly. Cut out a peony petal shape and place on a plastic tulip petal or similar veiner to make the veining pronounced, as shown. Eight petals are needed.

Frill the edges of the petals with a cocktail stick (toothpick) and place over a former, as shown.

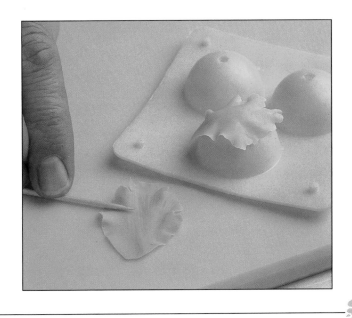

continued overleaf

PEONY
continued

Stick the petals on to the calyx, taking care that you do not brush egg white on to the ring. Position the petals with a slight overlap. As shown in the photograph, the calyx should be visible through the thin paste.

Arrange the first five petals in a circle and then place the remaining three petals on top. Refer to the photograph for positioning. Prop some pieces of foam rubber under the petals to give some movement to the flower and to give space between the petals.

Roll out some more pink-coloured flower paste and cut out seven smaller petals. Vein and frill as for the larger ones. Place four in position, with the remaining three on top. Support these petals with more foam rubber. Place some yellow stamens in the centre of the flower, as shown. Leave to dry.

Use a No4 round paintbrush and pink and peach dusting powders to achieve the soft shading needed for a peony.

If liked, make dark green glossy leaves; these provide a good background for the shading.

If you intend to wire the flower, remember to make a hole through both the flower and calyx while they are still soft.

Tape the stamens on to a wire that has been pushed through the centre, sliding a cone of green-coloured paste down the back to secure the flower.

JAPANESE MAPLE

Acer

The Japanese maple is one of the few trees that is almost more widely known by its botanical name. With its constantly changing colours, the foliage is much prized by flower arrangers. The colour of the leaves shown here is perhaps unusual in sugarcraft but it blends extremely well with shades of rust, peach, yellow and cream. I have used them with chrysanthemums to decorate the fan-shaped cake shown on page 53, but they could equally well be used on other celebration cakes, such as one for an autumn wedding.

JAPANESE MAPLE

EQUIPMENT

paste colours and dusting powders

green-covered wires

maple leaf veiner

porcupine quill or veining tool

former

brown florist's tape

Colour some white flower paste with brown, red and flesh paste colours to achieve the shade shown here. Squash a ball of paste between your thumb and first finger and roll out two-thirds thinly, leaving the remaining third thicker. Roll this from the centre outwards to retain a tubular shape for the wire.

Cut out the leaf shape and insert a piece of hooked 30g wire that has been dipped in egg white into the thicker part of the paste, as shown. Place on a maple leaf veiner or one with a fan type of veining. Then mark a vein down the centre of the leaf with a porcupine quill or veining tool.

Dry over a former, as shown. If you do not have a suitable one, you can make one from aluminium foil or use an ice ball tray. Leave to dry.

Brush the leaves with plum and yellow dusting powders to give them a natural shading, as shown. It is important that you use a flat brush so as to apply the correct intensity of colour. Then brush the leaves with vegetable fat to give them a natural gloss.

Use ¼-width brown florist's tape to wrap round the wires to make the brown stems. Then use more brown tape to attach the stems to a piece of 26g wire to make the main stem, as shown in the main photograph.

CELEBRATION CAKE

A delicate spray of chrysanthemums and Japanese maple decorates this cake made in the shape of a fan.

CHRYSANTHEMUM

Chrysanthemum

The chrysanthemum is the emblem of the Japanese Imperial family. There are many different varieties including the daisy, spider, incurved and pompom. The range of colours makes them very useful in sugarcraft. I mixed brown, yellow and flesh paste colours to achieve the rust shade shown here. I have used white chrysanthemums as the main flower on a Christmas cake as a change from the more familiar poinsettia or Christmas rose. Yellow ones are effective on a golden wedding cake. Chrysanthemums can be wired in groups or used on wires on their own.

EQUIPMENT

green-covered wire

paste colours and dusting powders

small, medium and large daisy cutters

modelling knife or scalpel

small ball tool

Dip a piece of hooked 26g green-covered wire in egg white and insert into a tiny ball of rust-coloured flower paste. Roll out some more of this paste very thinly and cut out three petals, using a small daisy cutter. Cut each petal in half lengthwise with a modelling knife or scalpel. Stick one on top of the other and cup the petals with a small ball tool.

Brush a little egg white on to the tiny ball of paste and thread the wire through the throat. Press firmly together. Move the petals around with a cocktail stick (toothpick) to give a round, spiky shape. Leave to dry.

Roll out some more paste and cut out one medium daisy petal shape. Roll a cocktail stick over each petal to give some movement. Cup and stick on to the back of the dry central piece, brushing egg white on to the back of the flower, not on to the petal.

Roll out some ivory-coloured and rust-coloured pastes to about 1.5mm (1/16in) thickness. Place the rust piece on top of the ivory and continue rolling out until very thin. Then cut out two medium and four large two-tone petals.

Roll a cocktail stick over the medium petals, vein each one down the centre and stick one on top of the other, overlapping. Stick on to the back of the flower. Do the same with two of the large petals. Cup each petal, stick together and stick on to the back of the flower.

Roll the remaining two petals with a cocktail stick. Vein and curl each petal, then cut each one in half making four petals, each looking like four fingers in a fan shape. Stick two in position, as shown. Place the remaining two in the opposite direction so as to cover the space around the wire.

Attach a calyx, cut with a medium daisy cutter, over the small bare square at the back. Flick the petals with the tip of your index finger to make them curve into the centre. Leave to dry.

Dust a little green dusting powder into the centre to give a slight shading.

IRIS

Iris

The Boy's Festival is traditionally celebrated each May with arrangements of iris, denoting an 'instinct for healthy growth and great righteousness'. The numerous varieties of iris range from large flowers on 1.20-metre (4-ft) stems to miniature Alpine iris. The small water iris shown here is made with a daffodil cutter. A bearded iris can be made with a tulip cutter following the same principles. Iris can be made with individual petals but I find those made with this cutter just as effective. The main photograph shows the flowers assembled for the cake on page 59.

EQUIPMENT

paste colours and dusting powders
green-covered wire
dog bone tool
green florist's tape
daffodil cutter
paintbrush
semolina, ground rice or maize meal
sweetcorn (mealie) leaf veiner

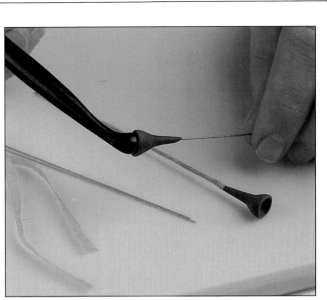

Mould a pea-sized piece of grey/green-coloured flower paste into a cone. Insert a piece of hooked 26g wire that has been dipped in egg white into the tapered end. Mould the paste round and then make a cavity with a dog bone tool, as shown. Tape two more pieces of 26g wire to the original piece using ⅓-width green florist's tape to make the stem. Leave to dry.

Colour some paste with a mixture of blue and violet paste colours. Roll out and cut out a daffodil petal shape. Soften the edge with a cocktail stick (toothpick) and vein down the centre of each petal on one side. Turn over and cup each petal from the outside to the inside. Turn over again so that the veins are on top and cup the centre firmly, as shown, so each petal curves.

Brush a little egg white into the dry cupped calyx and place the petal in position, as shown, making sure it is secure. Allow this to dry standing up so that the petals fall inwards.

After the first petal has dried for at least 30 minutes, roll out another. Frill, vein, turn over and cup as before but on the non-veined side. Position in the centre of the other petal overlapping so these

continued overleaf

IRIS
continued

petals sit in between the gaps of the first ones. Hang upside down in a glass so these petals all turn inwards towards the centre, as shown. Leave to dry.

When dry, brush with some violet dusting powder to remove any cornflour (cornstarch) marks and protect the flower from fading. The paste will fade but the dusting powder will not. This gives the iris a nice velvety look. Then brush a little white dusting powder quite softly on the top three petals in a line, using a No 2 or No 3 brush.

Brush a little egg white in a thin pennant shape on each of the bottom three petals and sprinkle some yellow-coloured semolina, ground rice or maize meal on to the egg white. Use a mixture of yellow and egg yellow dusting powders to get this rich shade. Brush off any excess.

Roll out some green/grey-coloured flower paste and cut out between five and nine pennant shapes, as shown, ranging from 2.5–6cm (1–2½in). Vein each one down the centre with a cocktail stick.

Starting with the smallest one, stick the first three pennants in between the petals to cover up the calyx. Roll the base where they meet the stem into a tubular shape so that the calyx and wire are completely covered by these bracts.

Cut out the leaves free-hand in long thin tapered strips. Vein on a sweetcorn (mealie) leaf veiner and dry flat. Brush with vegetable fat.

The two buds are made by inserting a hooked wire in a cone, then marking with a porcupine quill. Place some petals over the cone for the larger bud to give the effect of it opening.

IRIS CAKE

A cluster of small water iris is arranged on a bed of sugarpaste pebbles in the curve of this cake.

MAGNOLIA

Magnolia

Flower arrangement has only become an essential part of the education of Japanese girls in the last century. Before then, this formal art was only practised by men who are still the principal teachers. The different species of magnolia grow in many shapes, sizes and colours – some with six petals, others with nine or more. The spray shown here looks dramatic laid on top of a cake as the only decoration. If making a dark plum and white Chinese-type magnolia, the flower pastes are rolled out together as described on page 54 for the chrysanthemum.

EQUIPMENT

paste colours and dusting powders
green-covered wires
fine embroidery scissors
yellow cotton for stamens
rose leaf veiner
plastic tulip petal

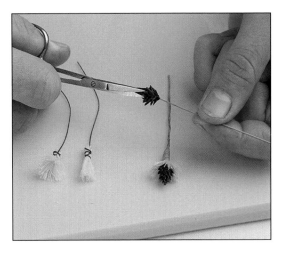

Colour some flower paste with a mixture of moss green and black paste colours to achieve the dark shade. Dip a piece of hooked 26g green-covered wire in egg white and insert into the thicker end of the cone. Using fine embroidery scissors, make tiny spikes all over the cone, working from the bottom to the top, as shown.

Wind some yellow cotton around your index finger about 50 times. Wrap wire round one folded end (see page 17). Cut off the excess cotton, squash down the centre and pull the cone through to rest on it like an egg on a nest. Tape the two together to secure, as shown.

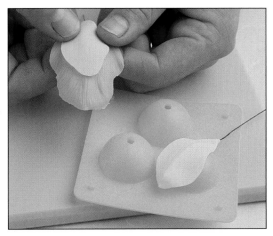

Roll out some dark green-coloured paste, retaining a thin tube at one end for the wire. Cut out the leaf shape with the square end from the thicker part of the paste. Insert a piece of hooked 30g wire that has been dipped in egg white into the leaf. Place on a rose leaf veiner and then roll a cocktail stick (toothpick) along the edge to give a soft frill. Place over a former to dry in a natural position. Three leaves are needed, one large and two slightly smaller ones.

Roll out some white paste, retaining a thin tube at one end. Cut out the petal. Insert a piece of hooked 30g wire that has been dipped in egg white into the thicker part and mould around the wire. Place on a plastic tulip petal or similar veiner, as shown. Lay the petal on a piece of foam rubber and vein the back to give reverse veining on the main side.

Brush a little egg white on to the top of the petal and stick together. Trim off excess paste with scissors to make a cup-shaped petal. Place on a former to dry. Make six petals using this method and one smaller one, made in the same way, veined down the centre but not cupped. Leave to dry.

Dust the big and the small petals with pink dusting powder, covering about two-thirds on the main side and just a line on the inside. Dust the end of the stamen cotton with pink too.

Tape three petals, as shown, and one taped in between with the smaller petal at the base in whatever position you like; in the main photograph it is shown on the right-hand side at the bottom. Tape the three leaves on to some wire to make the branches and then tape in the flower, bending it at a right angle so it sits correctly.

AUSTRA-LASIA

The vast continent of Australia is very sparsely populated compared with New Zealand. Large parts of the interior are desert or semi-desert, where spiny acacia and stunted eucalyptus struggle to survive. It is therefore surprising that Australia's wild flowers should be so spectacular; there are so many thousands of species that the task of cataloguing them all will not be completed for many more years.

New Zealand lies in one of the most unstable parts of the earth's crust and volcanic activity is a major feature of the North Island. Many of the traditional English spring flowers such as daffodils grow in profusion on the South Island, while the flora of the North Island is more Mediterranean in character.

Cake decorating is very popular in Australasia and a distinctive style has been developed. A lot of ribbon and tulle is combined with sugar flowers to give a very soft effect. The flowers are often not any particular variety – just, say, peach- or pink-coloured blossom. Fine embroidery, lace and extension work are popular as the focal points of a design.

Most people in Australasia are of British descent and they continue many of the customs of the old country. The more predictable weather allows many wedding receptions to be held in the garden of the bride's parents. As in England, two- or three-tier cakes are usually made for weddings. The one that I designed for this region features flowers and foliage from both Australia and New Zealand, so it would be very appropriate if the bride came from one country and the groom from the other.

WILD CLEMATIS

Clematis

Several clematis are native to New Zealand, including this large white variety. The Maoris named it *puawananga*, meaning 'flowers of the spirit'. The flowers can be seen climbing up trees and draped over fences. The ones shown here are about half life-size and can be used in sprays on wedding and other celebration cakes. The principle of drying the flowers in the calyx can be adapted to many other flowers including daisies. The calyx points support the flower while it is drying, thus avoiding the necessity of using any other supports.

EQUIPMENT

paste colour and dusting powders

small calyx cutter

green-covered wires

ball tool

fine veiner

white cotton stamens

porcupine quill

rose leaf veiner

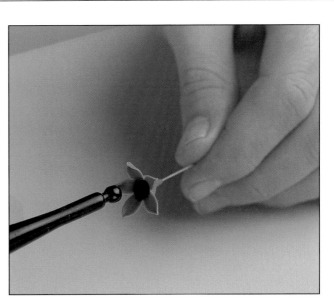

Make some green-coloured flower paste into a small cone and roll into a Mexican hat shape. Cut out a small calyx. Dip a piece of hooked 26g green-covered wire in egg white and insert into the base of the calyx. Mould around to secure.

Make a cavity with a ball tool, as shown. By bending the points of the calyx in various angles, you can achieve the effect of the flowers at different stages of opening on one spray. Leave to dry.

Roll out some white flower paste very thinly. Cut out seven petals. (Some flowers have only six petals.) Place on a fine veiner. Then vein down the centre of each petal and cup slightly to give some movement. Stick the petals on to the calyx with a little egg white, as shown.

Cut off the ends of about 20 white cotton stamens and wire around the base. Bend some of the stamens downwards at right angles to form a base and leave some upright, as shown. Dust green and plum dusting powders on the tips and stick in the central cavity with egg white.

Dust a mixture of yellow/green dusting powders around the centre of the flower, as shown. Make the buds from a cone marked with a porcupine quill and then stick a calyx on the back. Attach leaves made in dark green-coloured paste to 30g wire and vein on a rose leaf veiner.

SILVER FERN

Cyathea dealbata

Silver fern also grows in Australia but it is more common in New Zealand, where it is even used as the emblem of the renowned All Blacks rugby team. This fern has a silvery-green shading which looks good with most colours. I have used some silver fern on the Australasian wedding cake on page 63 as it is so attractive mixed with other flowers and foliage. A frond is shown in the main photograph in a piece of coral that I brought back from the Southern Hemisphere.

EQUIPMENT

paste colours and dusting powder
paintbrush
green-covered wire
leaf veiner
former

Colour some white flower paste with a mixture of green, black and blue paste colours. Roll out the paste, leaving a thicker part which is then rolled with a paintbrush, keeping a thin sausage shape in the centre, as shown, for the wire. Cut out the leaf.

Dip a piece of hooked 30g green-covered wire in egg white and insert into the thicker end of the leaf shape. Mould around the wire to secure the leaf. Place on a leaf veiner, similar to this leaf or a rose leaf, to vein. Roll a cocktail stick (toothpick) over the edge to give some movement to the leaf, as shown.

Place on a former so that the leaf will dry in a natural shape and not flat, as shown. Alternatively, you can use some crumpled tissue paper or kitchen foil.

When dry, brush over each leaf with white dusting powder. Then brush or spray with vegetable fat to give a silvery effect with the white underneath.

The leaves can be wired into fronds or used in single or double pieces in sprays.

DAPHNE

Daphne

During its flowering season this shrub is covered with clusters of dainty flowers, shaded pink to plum. Daphne grows abundantly in New Zealand. On my last trip there, one was growing outside my bedroom window in Hamilton and I can still remember its wonderful fragrance after the early morning dew had disappeared and the sun had come out. The flowers can be used singly or in clusters as they grow naturally. I have included some daphne among the flowers decorating the wedding cake I designed for this region, shown on page 63.

EQUIPMENT

paste colours and dusting powders
green-covered wire
paintbrush
daphne cutter
veining tool
tweezers
yellow stamens

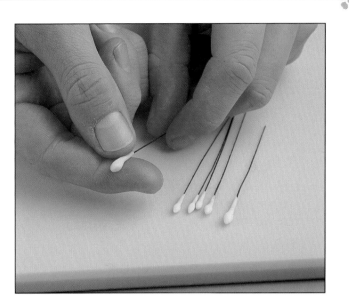

Mould a pea-sized ball of white flower paste into a cone. Dip a piece of hooked 30g wire in egg white and insert into the tapered end. Mould between your thumb and first finger to make the bud shape. Roll the ends to a slight point, as shown. For a cluster, between five and nine buds in assorted sizes are needed.

Make a piece of white flower paste into a small toadstool shape. Roll with a paint-brush, as shown, to thin the base part. Using a daphne cutter, cut out a daphne shape with its four petals. Make a hole in the centre. Mark two opposite petals with veins just inside the edge.

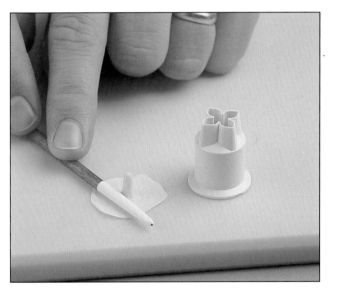

Dip a piece of hooked 30g wire in egg white and thread through the throat and mould securely. Using tweezers, place a small yellow stamen in the hole and leave to dry.

Dust the backs of the flowers and the tips of the buds with pink/plum dusting pow-der, using a No3 or No4 brush. Then dust green on the base of the flowers and buds and into the centres. Finally dust some pearly snowflake dusting powder all over with a No4 brush to give the slight sheen a daphne has.

Make leaves, if wished, in apple green-coloured flower paste, attach to 30g wire and leave to dry. Then paint with dark green paste colour mixed with clear spirit, leaving the main lateral vein apple green.

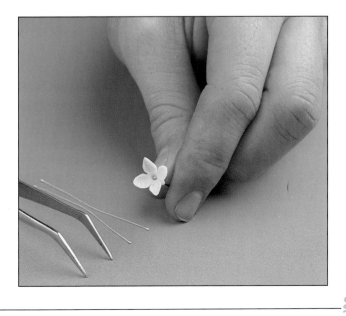

ARUM LILY

Richardia aethiopica

Knowing how expensive a single bloom can be in an English florist, I was amazed by the enormous numbers of arum lilies growing by the wayside in New Zealand in July. They like moist soil and thrive near a stream. With the fashion for more dramatic or even coloured wedding dresses, arum lilies have become almost as familiar in bridal bouquets as pink roses and gypsophila. The large cone-shaped flowers look very striking made in sugar and are best used on their own in a simple spray or an *ikebana*-type arrangement.

EQUIPMENT

paste colours and dusting powder
template or arum lily cutter
green-covered wire
semolina, ground rice or maize meal
plastic tulip petal
veining tool
paintbrushes

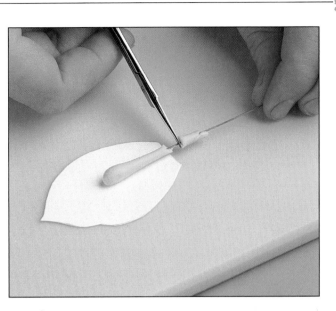

Mould a ball of yellow-coloured flower paste into a long thin cone. Dip a piece of hooked 26g green-covered wire in egg white and insert into the tapered end, pushing deeply into the paste to support the cone. Lay the cone over the template or cutter and trim off any excess, as shown, to make a spadix about half the length of the spathe. Taper the thin end slightly. Tape two more pieces of 26g wire to the original piece.

Brush some egg white over the spadix and dip in yellow-coloured semolina, ground rice or maize meal, leaving about one-eighth plain at the base where the spathe is attached, as shown.

Roll out some white flower paste; as the arum lily has thick spathes, do not roll the paste out as thinly as usual. Using a template or cutter, cut out the spathe shape and place on a plastic tulip petal or similar veiner. Then mark a vein down the centre.

Brush some egg white round the base of the spathe and place the spadix in the centre. Bring the right-hand side of the spathe over, as shown, and roll to wrap the base tightly, as shown. Bend the end over. Leave to dry.

Brush green dusting powder around the base of the flower, on the top of the spathe and around the spadix, using a No3 or No4 round brush. Finally, using a clean brush, brush vegetable fat over the flower to give the natural waxy appearance.

WARATAH

Telopea speciosissima

The waratah is the floral emblem of the state of New South Wales. Its botanical name is derived from the word *telopas*, meaning 'seen at a distance'. This is an allusion to the great distances from which the crimson flowers can be seen in spring. Waratah has great beauty and distinction; it is very rarely seen in flower outside its native habitat. It could be used as the focal point in an arrangement of Australian wild or native flowers on a celebration cake, perhaps for a ruby wedding or Christmas.

EQUIPMENT

paste colours and dusting powder
green-covered wire
green florist's tape
paintbrushes
sweetcorn (mealie) leaf veiner
cake pillar
tweezers

Mould a piece of red-coloured flower paste into the shape of a medium-sized strawberry, as shown.

Tape three pieces of 26g green-covered wire together with green florist's tape and bend one end into a circle, as shown. Brush this end with egg white and push into the base of the strawberry shape. Mould around the back to secure.

Use the end of a paintbrush to make holes all over the surface of the strawberry shape for the terminal head parts.

Roll some red-coloured flower paste first into tiny balls, as shown, then into long, thin, bulbous-ended tubes.

Starting from the tapered end of the strawberry shape, stick the thinner ends of the tubes into the holes made with the paintbrush, as shown. Make the pieces a little longer as you work down towards the wire. Make sure that you squash all the pieces securely into the holes so that they will stay in position and not fall out when they are dry. Leave this terminal head to dry for about a day.

continued overleaf

WARATAH
continued

Cut out free-hand petal shapes in red-coloured flower paste for the bracts. Press each bract on to a sweetcorn (mealie) leaf veiner to vein it. Then stick to the terminal head with egg white. As this has now dried completely, you can squash the bracts into position without any fear that the terminal head will fall off the wire.

Then attach a second row of slightly larger bracts, as shown. About 11 are needed in all for each flower.

Support the flower in a cake pillar and use tweezers to tuck some pieces of foam rubber between each bract to create the open effect that the waratah has, as shown. Leave to dry.

Brush a little green dusting powder around the base of the bracts and on the top of the terminal head. Then brush with vegetable fat to give a natural gloss.

WATTLE

Acacia pycnantha

Growing extensively throughout the country, this member of the acacia family is appropriately Australia's national floral emblem. There are hundreds of species of acacias. In England the most usual variety is probably the one known as mimosa; this has fine feathery leaves and is mostly imported from the South of France in early spring. Wattle is quite quick to make and can be used on many types of celebration cakes. I have used some on the wedding cake (page 63) and on the rectangular birthday cake overleaf.

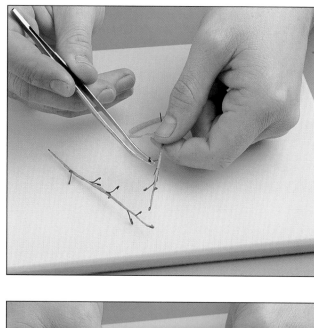

WATTLE

EQUIPMENT

paste colours
florist's tape
green-covered wires
tweezers
semolina, ground rice or maize meal

Tape some pieces of 30g green-covered wire to a piece of 26g wire to make 'branches' of whatever length you like from about 1cm (½in) long. Make as many as you wish. When they are all taped, bend a hook on the end of each piece of wire with tweezers, as shown.

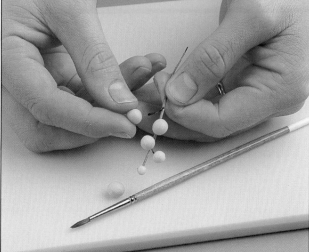

Roll some yellow-coloured flower paste into balls of graduated sizes. Brush the wire hooks with a little egg white and attach the balls of paste, using the larger ones towards the base, as shown. Brush over with some egg white and sprinkle some dark yellow-coloured semolina, ground rice or maize meal over the balls of paste, as shown. Leave to dry.

The wattle can be wired into sprays. To make the leaves, cut these out free-hand from flower paste coloured with a mixture of green, black and blue paste colours to match the grey-green colour of the wattle leaf. Attach the leaves to 30g wire.

The leaves in the photograph were veined on fresh wattle leaves to produce the correct veining. If you like, you can cut round the fresh leaves to use as templates, thus obtaining the exact shape and size.

BRUCE'S CAKE

A kangaroo has been painted on this birthday cake. A pattern for making a template is given on page 144.

BORONIA

Boronia

The flowers of this evergreen shrub, which is a native of Australia, are quick and simple to make. As no cutters are required, the flowers can be made in whatever size you wish. They can be used on their own to decorate a small celebration cake, or combined as fillers with other Australian wild or cultivated flowers in a spray. I have used several buds to add more realism to the spray shown in the main photograph. The feathery foliage is made from florist's tape.

EQUIPMENT

paste colours and dusting powder
green-covered wires
modelling tool or wooden dowel
modelling knife or scalpel
green florist's tape

Mould a pearl-sized ball of yellow/cream-coloured flower paste into a small cone. Dip a piece of hooked 30g or 33g green-covered wire in egg white and insert into the base of the cone. Mould into a bud shape, as shown. Between five and nine buds are needed for each spray.

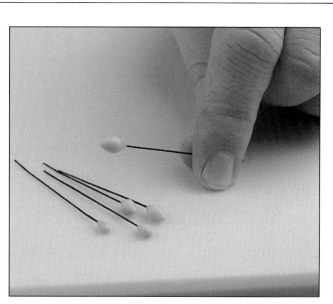

Mould a pea-sized piece of yellow/cream-coloured flower paste into a cone. Insert a modelling tool or wooden dowel into the base to cup the flower. Cut four petals with a modelling knife or scalpel, dividing the cone into equal-sized quarters, as shown. Squash and pinch each petal to give it a rounded shape. Place on a piece of foam rubber and cup each petal so that it curves inwards.

Thread a piece of hooked 30g green-covered wire that has been dipped in egg white down through the throat of the flower, as shown. Press the paste securely around the hook. Mark a small line down the base of each petal to form a cross in the centre. Leave to dry.

Dust some green dusting powder into the centre of each flower. Paint the backs of the flowers a reddish colour, using paste colours mixed with clear spirit. Emphasize the cross in the centre by painting this with the same colour.

Wire the buds and flowers on to a piece of 26g wire, adding the foliage as you work. The foliage is made from green florist's tape cut in tiny feathery pieces. This gives a very natural effect that can also be used for other flowers such as heathers (*ericas*).

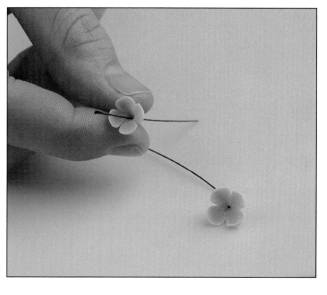

MAIDENHAIR FERN

Adiantum

In many parts of the world today maidenhair fern is a popular house plant. Every conservatory in England in Victorian times would have several pots of this fern; the cooks working in the grander houses would frequently ask the gardener for some sprays to decorate the elaborate cream puddings favoured in those days. You will need to grow a maidenhair fern as the dried stems are used. Like gypsophila, it is a soft, dainty foliage to mix with some of the larger sugar flowers.

EQUIPMENT

paste colour
flower press or heavy book
fine veiner
paintbrush

Cut as many pieces of maidenhair fern as you want to reproduce in sugar. Leave in a flower press or in an old heavy book for about a week to dry. Then cut off all the leaves, except for a tiny triangular piece, as shown, at the base.

Roll out some green-coloured flower paste really thinly. Cut out the leaves, as shown. You will need an assortment of different sizes for each frond. Place on a fine veiner, then frill the edges with a cocktail stick (toothpick), as shown.

Mix some of the green-coloured flower paste with a little egg white to make a glue of the consistency of royal icing. Brush a little on to the end of a stem of the dried maidenhair fern and stick a leaf on top. It will set very quickly.

In the photographs I am working on a board for better contrast, but when doing this at home, I use a piece of waxed (wax) paper so that any excess glue will peel off easily and not stick to the board. Leave to dry.

Mix some green paste colour with a little clear spirit and paint over the leaves to give them a shaded effect. Leave to dry.

An alternative way of making this fern is to make a fan shape in 33g wire and stick the leaves on to this instead of the stems. This method is ideal both in humid climates where the dried stems would go soft in the moist atmosphere or if you do not have any real maidenhair fern available.

EPIDENDRUM ORCHID

Epidendrum

This dainty little orchid grows wild in Australasia and the South Pacific. Like the oncidium orchid (page 38) it is useful wired into sprays on smaller cakes or used as a filler with larger orchids such as the cymbidium. It is fairly time-consuming to make and, to achieve the same impact as a larger orchid, you need several. In sugarcraft epidendrums are often known as the poor man's orchid although this is not strictly correct since that variety is a little different. However, it can be helpful to think of the epidendrum in terms of a matchstick man!

EQUIPMENT

paste colours and dusting powders

epidendrum cutters

modelling knife or scalpel

green-covered wire

veining tool

Roll out some flesh/red-coloured flower paste, leaving it thicker at one end, as shown. The shape of the cutter resembles a man with a rounded head and square limbs. Use the cutter so that the head is cut from the thicker part of the paste.

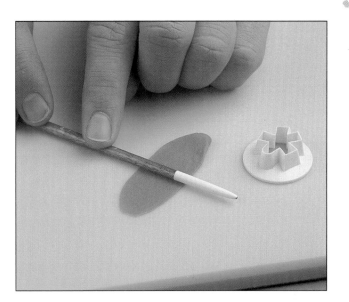

Roll the arms and legs slightly to make them thinner than the body. Use a modelling knife or scalpel to make the feathery pieces on the arms and legs. Hollow the head slightly with a cocktail stick (toothpick). Dip a piece of hooked 26g green-covered wire in egg white and insert into the head. Draw the sides round and roll into a long thin tube.

Place a small pointed piece of paste in the centre to form the pollen tract. Split a small ball of yellow-coloured flower paste in two and place at the top for the stigma, with two tiny balls on either side of the pollen tract to complete the central part of the flower, as shown.

Roll out some more paste for the back part. Cut out the sepals and petals in one piece, as shown. Vein each part and turn over. Again thinking of the shape as a matchstick man, cup three of the parts for the head and legs. Turn over again and cup the central part of the flower. Thread this on to the tubular section, so that half of this protrudes at the back, as shown. Leave to dry.

Dust red dusting powder all over the petals and sepals, and around the feathery parts of the throat; some white around the pollen tract and green around the stigma. Mix a little red paste colour with clear spirit and paint a few spots, as shown in the main photograph.

POINSETTIA

Euphorbia pulcherrima

In Australasia and parts of Africa poinsettias grow into magnificent trees with literally hundreds of blooms. Smaller varieties are very popular in many countries as house plants at Christmas time, in shades of cream, coral pink and particularly the vivid red shown here. It is the bracts framing the central flower that make poinsettias look so dramatic. A poinsettia takes rather a long time to make in sugar but it makes an appropriate decoration for a Christmas cake like the one shown overleaf.

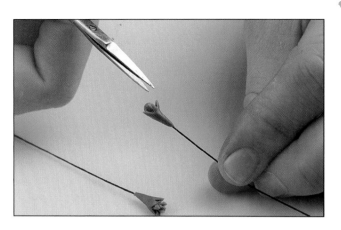

EQUIPMENT

paste colours and dusting powders

green-covered wires

fine embroidery scissors

wooden dowel

Make a small ball of green-coloured flower paste into a cone. Dip a piece of hooked 30g green-covered wire in egg white and insert into the tapered end of the cone. Holding fine embroidery scissors at the angle shown, snip the cone to make little hairs. Nine such cones are needed for each central flower.

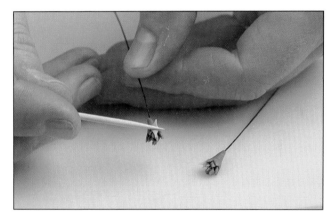

Roll a minute ball of yellow-coloured flower paste into a tube with pointed ends. Roll this on your finger with a cocktail stick (toothpick) and place in position on the side of the flower. (When I am teaching this flower, I call this part a rooster as it looks like one with its beak and comb sticking up.) Repeat this step with the remaining eight flowers.

Mix some red paste colour with clear spirit and paint over the small cut pieces on the flowers. Then mix white and yellow dusting powders with clear spirit to get a creamy yellow colour. Paint this over the red parts to provide shading.

To make the bracts, roll out some red-coloured flower paste, retaining a thin tubular shape for the wire. Dip a piece of hooked 30g wire in egg white and insert into the tubular shape. Mould around the wire securely. Soften the edge of the bract with a paintbrush or cocktail stick. Vein down the centre, as shown below.

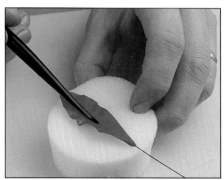

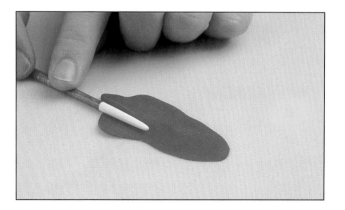

continued overleaf

POINSETTIA
continued

Follow the same principle to make four smaller bracts of different sizes, as shown. Lay all five sets of bracts over a wooden dowel to give slight shaping while drying.

Repeat this step to make a further ten bracts of varying sizes and three green-coloured bracts, but attach these to 26g wire. Because red usually takes longer to dry than most other colours, allow a day for drying.

Assemble the poinsettia, as shown, by first taping three of the flowers (small rooster shape) together. Bend the red bracts at right angles to make it easier to tape them. Make a fan shape from one of each size of the red bracts, taping one to the right, then one to the left, then right, then left, then right and finally a green bract to the left. Follow this sequence with the remaining bracts, thus making three such sections. Tape these together firmly.

The bracts can then be bent to achieve a well-shaped poinsettia. As the green bracts are thicker, remember to use tweezers to bend these. Some poinsettias have only one or two red bracts, so if you are making a spray, you could vary the number of red bracts to make it look more natural.

CHRISTMAS CAKE

The white icing of the trefoil-shaped cake makes an effective contrast to the red poinsettia. Holly berries and miniature Christmas roses in each indentation are linked by a swag of red sugarpaste.

SOUTH PACIFIC

The exotic flowers, beautiful beaches and warm sea make the islands of Fiji and Hawaii idyllic places to stop on the long flight from Australasia to North America. The scents of frangipani, gardenia and stephanotis are almost overwhelming in their intensity, particularly after a tropical shower. The avenues of flame trees to be found in many Fijian towns and villages are a breathtaking sight in spring. Many kinds of tropical fruit grow abundantly in Fiji but sugar cane and coconut palms are by far the most important crops.

In Fiji it is customary for every branch of the family to receive a cake at the wedding feast. When I was in New Zealand, a bride from Fiji had just ordered a 29-tier cake that would have to be displayed on various stands on the day.

Hawaii became the 50th state of the Union in 1959. It is known as the Aloha state, *aloha* being the Hawaiian word for both greetings and farewell. *Leis* are given to visitors on arrival in Hawaii as a sign of welcome. Another *lei* is presented on departure; this is traditionally tossed on to the harbour waters. If the garland drifts back to the shore, it indicates that the traveller will some day return to the islands.

The hibiscus on the two-tier wedding cake are shown in three vibrant colours. I reproduced some of the shells and coral I had brought back from the South Pacific to decorate the tops of the cakes, with some of the small clown fish that swim in enormous shoals in the ocean. The cake could be placed on semolina coloured to resemble sand. This design would also be appropriate in other tropical areas such as the Caribbean islands.

HIBISCUS

Rosa sinensis

Also known as rose-mallow, the hibiscus family has many hybrid varieties. In some countries it is a popular house plant but in Hawaii it grows in the form of a large shrub. As the blooms will last a full day after picking before they wilt, they are often chosen to decorate Hawaiian girls' hair for festive occasions. Some varieties can stain clothing so they are not used in the traditional *leis*. The range of colours includes shades of red, orange and yellow. The flowers look spectacular made in sugar to decorate celebration cakes.

EQUIPMENT

paste colour and dusting powders
green-covered wires
plastic tulip petal
porcupine quill or veining tool
curved former
cranked tweezers
small yellow stamens
miniature stamens
semolina, ground rice or maize meal

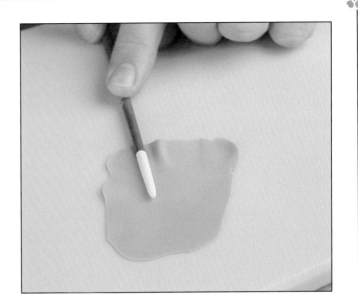

To make each petal, roll some pink-coloured flower paste into a medium-sized ball and flatten this between your thumb and first finger. Roll out two-thirds of the paste thinly with a rolling pin into a petal shape. Five petals are needed.

Use a paintbrush to roll out the remaining third of the paste, working from the centre outwards on both sides and keeping a small sausage-shaped ridge, as shown, in the centre to secure the wire.

Dip a piece of hooked 28g green-covered wire in a little egg white. Insert the hooked end of the wire into the ridged part of the petal. Mould the paste around the wire to ensure it is securely attached. Repeat with the remaining petals.

Press each petal gently on to a plastic tulip petal or similar, heavily veined, former. Mark the central veins of each petal with a porcupine quill or veining tool, as shown.

Roll a paintbrush or cocktail stick (toothpick) gently around the edge of each petal to make a soft frill. Lay each petal over a curved former, as shown; if you do not have a suitable one, use an inverted egg carton. Leave until the petals are absolutely dry.

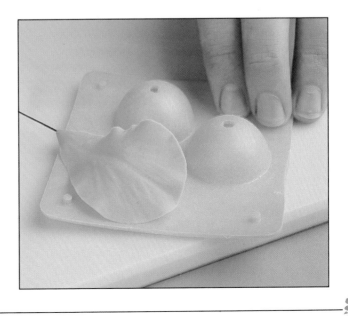

continued overleaf

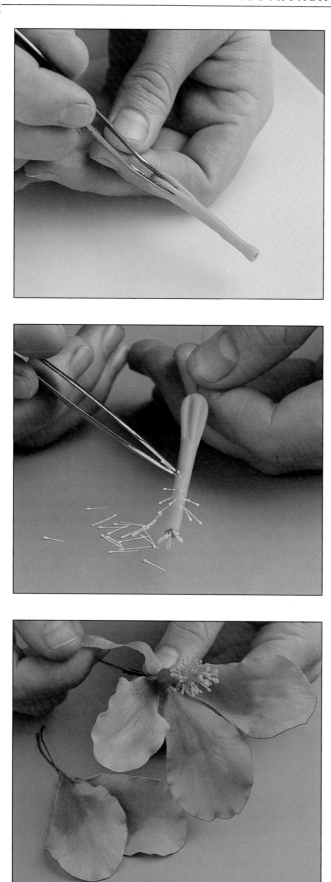

HIBISCUS
continued

Roll a ball of pink-coloured flower paste into a sausage shape about the same length as the petals. Dip a piece of hooked 26g green wire in a little egg white. Push the wire through the centre of the sausage shape right up to the top to support it completely.

Then roll the top of the paste to taper it slightly and make a cavity in the tip with a paintbrush. Using plain cranked tweezers, pinch the paste to make five ridges, as shown.

Brush a little egg white into the top cavity and insert five small yellow stamens. Then insert 30–40 miniature stamens into the paste between the ridges and cavity, as shown. It is most important to do this immediately before the paste dries. If it has dried, make small holes with a porcupine quill for the stamens.

Push the wire into a piece of florist's foam and leave until the paste is dry.

When all the parts are dry, brush some pink dusting powder into the centre of each petal, using a flat brush so as to achieve an intense colour.

Brush the stigma and the tips of all the stamens with a little egg white and roll in some semolina, ground rice or maize meal that has been coloured with yellow dusting powder to give the effect of pollen on the stamens and stigma.

GARDENIA

Gardenia jasminoides

Sometimes called the cape jasmine, this flower looks like a large white rose with dark glossy green leaves. Gardenias grow in most tropical areas. The fragrant flowers are used in bouquets, corsages and *leis* but the petals bruise very easily. The fruits are used in a number of natural food dyes. A member of the same plant family called a *tiare* grows in Tahiti; this looks like a stephanotis with seven rounded petals and lime-green leaves and is also very strongly scented.

GARDENIA

EQUIPMENT

former
paste colours and dusting powders
calyx cutter
paintbrushes
porcupine quill

Grease a former with a little vegetable fat. Roll out some green-coloured flower paste and cut out a calyx. Place on the former.

Roll out some white flower paste very thinly and cut out six large petals. Soften the edges with a paintbrush and position as shown, bending towards the right. Prop up the petals with pieces of foam rubber.

Roll out some more white flower paste and cut out six medium-sized petals. Soften the edges and position as shown. Prop up these petals. Then cut out eight small petals and soften the edges.

Place three of the small petals on top of the medium-sized petals. Arrange the remaining five in a fan shape (see frangipani, page 96) and stick together with egg white. Roll into a cone and squash the base. Cut off a little of the thicker part, stick into the centre and then open up, using the end of a paintbrush to give a spiral effect. Prop up these petals.

Make the leaves in dark green-coloured flower paste. Use a porcupine quill to mark the main vein and smaller veins running from the centre outwards.

Mix some green and yellow dusting powder together with cornflour (cornstarch) to make a very pale colour. Dust this on to the top of the flower and on the base of the petals to give a slight shading, as shown. Brush the leaves with vegetable fat to make them glossy.

GARDENIA CAKE

A gardenia, framed by its glossy leaves, makes an elegant decoration combined with a trail of white ginger.

FRANGIPANI

Plumeria acutifolia

Usually known in Hawaii by its botanical name, frangipani has a beautiful scent. It is also called a temple flower as the blooms are often placed before altars in temples. Once picked, the flowers only last for about eight hours but are probably more frequently used than any other in *leis* in the South Pacific and the Hawaiian islands. Most frangipani is white, although some flowers are yellow or shades of red. As its gardenia-like leaves are very large in proportion to the flowers, they would not normally be made in sugar.

EQUIPMENT

paste colours and dusting powder

cake pillar or liqueur or sherry glass

round paintbrush

Roll out some white flower paste and cut out five petals. Roll each petal as shown so that a curved lip is formed on the left-hand side of each one. Stick the petals together with egg white in a fan shape, as shown.

Brush a little egg white down the edge of the base of the right-hand petal and bring the left-hand petal over to meet it, forming a cone, as shown. Hold this upside down and twist the base into a spiral to secure the petals.

Place in a cake pillar or a liqueur or sherry glass filled with cornflour (cornstarch) to support the flower while it is drying, as shown. Leave to dry, then brush off the excess cornflour.

Using a No4 round paintbrush, brush some yellow dusting powder into the throat of the flower to give the shading, as shown in the main photograph.

If you wish to wire the frangipani, make a small calyx in green-coloured flower paste, like the one used for the iris (page 56), and place the dry flower in the soft calyx, sticking with egg white.

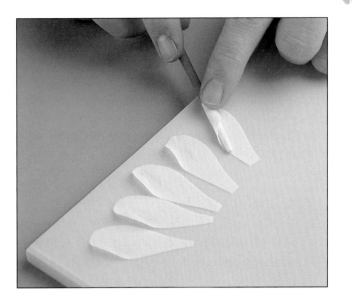

WHITE GINGER

Zingiber officinale

Like the gardenia and frangipani, white ginger also has a wonderful fragrance, particularly noticeable when one is dining outside on a warm summer evening. It is not surprising that it is used in some cosmetics based on natural products. Ginger is an important crop in Fiji and it is grown commercially for export. The orchid-like appearance of the flower makes it an unusual and interesting choice for decorating a wedding or other celebration cake. It must be emphasized that the sugar version is very fragile and can easily be damaged.

EQUIPMENT

paste colours and dusting powder
white and green-covered wires
fine veiner
veining tool
former
semolina, ground rice or semolina
green florist's tape

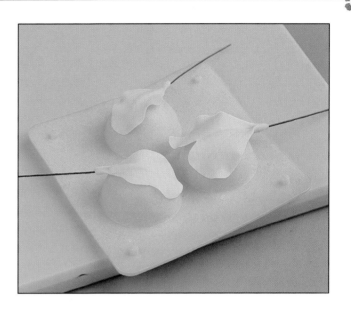

Roll out some white flower paste, retaining a thicker part for the wires. Cut out two wing petals and one sepal. Dip three pieces of hooked 30g green-covered wire in egg white and insert one into each part. Place on a fine veiner and soften the edges slightly with a paintbrush to frill very softly, as shown.

Mark a vein down the centre of the sepal. Turn the petals over and vein the backs to make inverted veining, as shown. Remember to vein one on one side, the other on the opposite side so that they will be a mirror image when assembled, not identical. Place on a former, as shown.

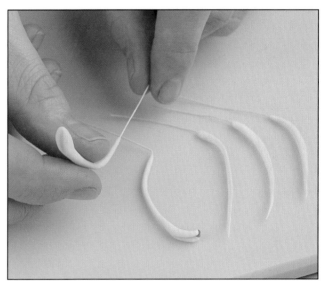

Mould some white flower paste into a thin sausage shape for the centre column. Dip a piece of hooked 30g white wire (to prevent a dark shadow) and push this right up the total length of the column to support it completely.

Make a mark on the top side with a veining tool. Brush a little egg white on the under-side and dip in some golden-brown-coloured semolina, ground rice or maize meal. Then stick a small ball of brown-coloured paste on the end and mark to split it in half, as shown.

Then roll out three long thin pieces, as shown. Stick a piece of hooked 30g white wire into the thicker end and vein down the centre. Place over a curved former to dry. Assemble as shown by taping the parts together. Using a No 3 or No 4 brush, dust with pale yellow dusting powder, taking care not to damage the long thin parts.

NORTH AMERICA

The American approach to cake decorating is very different from that of most other parts of the world. Fruit cakes are usually only made for Thanksgiving or Christmas. Marzipan and royal icing are comparatively seldom used to cover such cakes. They are normally left plain or decorated with candied fruits – sometimes in the shape of a flower or a bunch of cherries – and then glazed. Different types of sponge are by far the most popular cakes for celebrations. Some of the flavourings are quite distinctive such as Italian cream, kahlua cream, cherry chip and red velvet.

Most people think that the tiers of American-style wedding cakes are not separated by pillars but placed directly on top of each other in graduating sizes. In fact many different styles of stand are also used to display the cake. It is traditional for the bride to cut the first piece of the cake.

On a day when it is the bride who is the centre of attention, the American custom of having a special groom's cake is charming. This is almost invariably chocolate and the frosting used to cover the cake is a form of butter cream.

Rolled fondant or sugarpaste has started to become popular in North America. I have used this in a pale pink shade for the graduated heart-shaped cake shown here. It is decorated with dogwood and forget-me-not. A pattern for making a template for the small doves is given on page 144.

Coffee or punch is usually served with the cake and perhaps some dainty sandwiches. More substantial food is less frequently offered at wedding receptions.

MISTLETOE

Viscum album

The early European settlers in Virginia found plenty of mistletoe growing there, so they were able to continue the custom of hanging some in their homes at Christmas. Sprigs of mistletoe are still invariably tucked into the kissing balls hung from chandeliers, doorways and even outside lanterns in Williamsburg each festive season. Mistletoe is the state flower of Oklahoma. It makes an attractive spray on a Christmas cake and can be used either on its own or mixed with other seasonal flowers and foliage.

EQUIPMENT

paste colours and dusting powder

green-covered wires

florist's tape

paintbrush

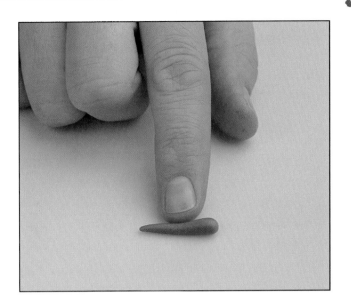

Roll a small thin cone of green-coloured flower paste between your thumb and first finger or on the work surface, as shown. Insert a piece of hooked 26g green-covered wire that has been dipped in egg white in the tapered end. Then roll, as shown, so that the leaf turns slightly to the right. Roll a second leaf to the left. Mark a vein down the centre of each leaf.

Make a cross from two pieces of 30g green-covered wire, twisting the horizontal wire around the vertical securely. Cover the twisted part with florist's tape. Trim the top piece of wire to about 1cm (½in) long and the two side pieces to about 6mm (¼in) long. Bend hooks on the end of each of these three pieces of wire.

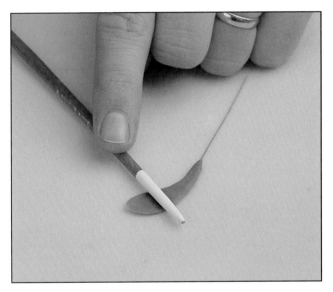

Colour some white flower paste very delicately with a little green paste colour and roll into four small balls. Stick one on each hook and the fourth on top of the others, using egg white. Mark a small cavity with a paintbrush on each berry.

Brush a little green dusting powder on to the leaves. Then brush with vegetable fat. Paint tiny green lines of food colouring on the berries and then brush with vegetable fat.

Two identical sprays have been taped together as shown in the photograph. Finally, stick a small green cone of paste in the centre of the 'V' of each leaf when the leaves are in the right position and mark with a porcupine quill or cocktail stick (toothpick) to form the cones.

FORGET-ME-NOT

Myosotis

Being so far away from the other states in the Union, it seems very appropriate that Alaska should have chosen the forget-me-not as its state flower. These dainty flowers are mostly in shades of blue but some varieties also have mauve and pink petals among the blue ones. Forget-me-nots were very popular in 19th-century English cottage gardens. They have a slightly old-fashioned quality that makes them perfect to use in decorating a cake for a Victorian-style wedding. They are also a suitable choice for a baby boy's christening cake.

EQUIPMENT

paste colours and dusting powders
green-covered wires
medium-sized blossom cutter
miniature ball tool or stylus
paintbrush
green florist's tape

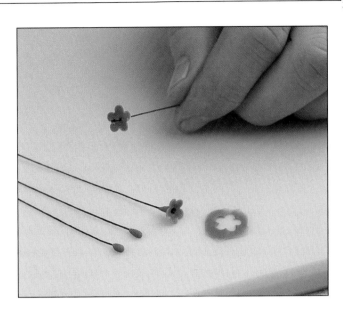

Colour some flower paste by mixing cream and blue paste colours together to make the powder blue shade, as shown. Dip a piece of hooked 33g wire in egg white and insert into a minute ball of paste to make the bud. Mould the paste securely to the wire.

Make the flower following the Mexican hat method, using a medium-sized blossom cutter. Make a hole in the centre with a cocktail stick (toothpick) and thread a piece of hooked 33g wire that has been dipped in egg white through the throat until the hook disappears, as shown.

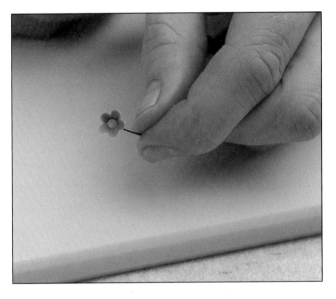

Using a miniature ball tool, a stylus or the end of a paintbrush, make a small cavity in the flower and stick a tiny ball of yellow-coloured flower paste in the centre, as shown. Squash this down until it is level with the tips of the petals.

Pull the paste from the outside inwards with a cocktail stick to make a miniature blossom shape. You must do this immediately before the paste dries. Make a hole in the centre with a cocktail stick.

Mix some white dusting powder with clear spirit and add some green paste colour. Paint a small calyx on the back of each bud and flower, also painting down the wires for about 2.5–5cm (1–2in). Leave to dry.

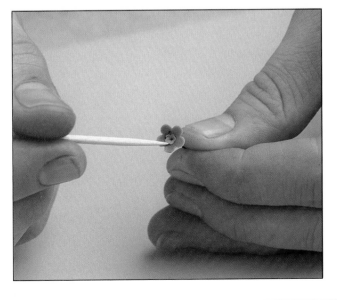

Assemble into sprays, starting with the buds. (Vary the number of flowers and buds on each spray.) Tape on to a piece of 30g wire. Then paint over the tape with the green colour used for the calyx. Forget-me-nots have pale foliage and stems; as fine wire is only available in dark green, it should be painted.

CACTI

Cacti

The desert area, known as the Saguaro National Monument, in the south-east of Arizona is a fascinating place to visit. Giant cacti as high as 15m (50ft) grow there. So many people cultivate smaller varieties of the cactus family as a hobby that I thought they would be most effective made in sugar to decorate an enthusiast's birthday cake. An original idea would be to cover the top of the cake with semolina, ground rice or maize meal, coloured to look like sand, and plant this with different types of cacti.

EQUIPMENT

paste colours
porcupine quill
modelling knife
plastic tulip veiner
stamens or cotton centre
paintbrushes
semolina, ground rice or maize meal

For the prickly cactus, roll a ball of green-coloured flower paste of whatever size you want the finished cactus. Mark with the end of a paintbrush and a porcupine quill to give the deep ridges, as shown.

Roll some cream-coloured flower paste into tiny tubular pieces pointed at both ends. These are the prickles. Mark in half with a porcupine quill or cocktail stick (toothpick) to fold and position wherever you want a cluster. Build up the small area with double and single pieces, as shown. Leave to dry.

Mix some brown paste colour with clear spirit and with a No2 paintbrush, paint over the prickles to give them shading, as shown.

continued overleaf

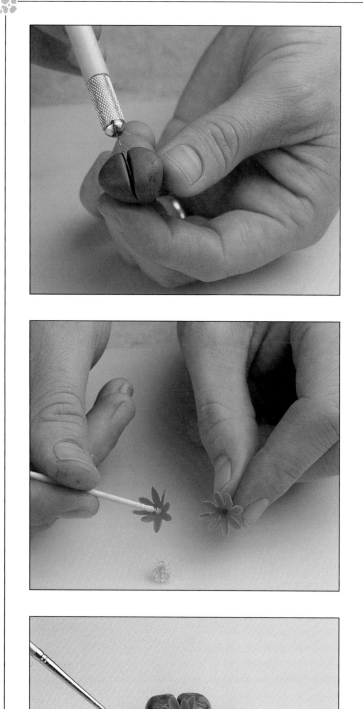

CACTI
continued

For the other cactus, called a living stone, colour some flower paste with black and brown paste colours to make the shade shown. Mould and cut with a modelling knife to split it open, as shown. Press the top on a plastic tulip veiner so as to get a slightly uneven top.

Make two daisy shapes in pink-coloured flower paste: one like a Mexican hat, the other flat. Vein the flat one down the centre and place in the cavity of the Mexican hat, sticking with egg white. Stick some stamens or a cotton centre in the centre.

Position the flower as shown in the cluster of cacti. These can be placed on a base to make it easier to position and stick them together. Brush some vegetable fat over the grey part. Then mix some pink paste colour with the fat and paint small lines, as shown, using a fine paintbrush.

The main photograph shows the pair of cacti. The sand is made from semolina, ground rice or maize meal, coloured to make it look like golden sand.

Using these basic principles, other varieties of cacti can be made. The addition of small labels made of flower paste denoting the variety would be a nice finishing touch on a cake.

BLACK-EYED SUSAN

Thunbergia

These cheerful orange flowers bring colour to many a back yard –
the usual prosaic-sounding term for a garden in the United States.
Comparatively few Americans are enthusiastic gardeners. Ironically, some
of the most spectacular gardens that I have seen are those created on the
terraces and flat roofs of apartment buildings in the major cities.
Black-eyed Susan can be used as a single flower or wired into a spray. A
novel way of using it is shown on the cake overleaf.

BLACK-EYED SUSAN

EQUIPMENT

paste colours and dusting powder
blossom and calyx cutters
wooden dowel
green-covered wires
maple leaf veiner

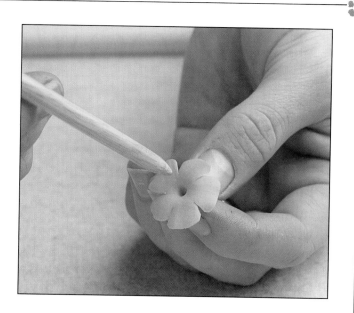

Make a Mexican hat shape from pale orange-coloured flower paste. Cut out with a blossom cutter. Cut a straight edge on each petal, as shown. Soften the edges with a cocktail stick (toothpick) and make a cavity in the centre with a wooden dowel, as shown. Dip a piece of hooked 26g green-covered wire in egg white and insert into the flower.

Roll out some green-coloured flower paste and cut out a small calyx. Stick on the back of the flower, as shown, with egg white. Leave to dry.

Dust the flower with orange dusting powder to give some shading. Mix some black paste colour with a little clear spirit and paint into the cavity and lightly on the top to make the black eye, as shown.

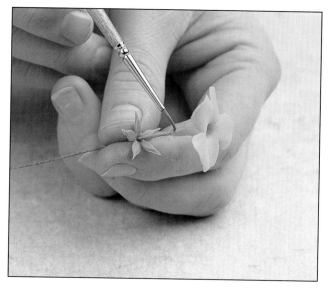

Make the leaves from mid-green-coloured flower paste and attach to 30g wire. Vein the leaves on a maple leaf veiner or one with a fan-type veining. Make the tendrils by wrapping 33g covered wires round a paintbrush to create a curly effect.

Use either 28g or 26g wire to make the flowers and leaves into a spray. The gauge of the wire depends on how pliable you want the spray to be. If it is to be wound round a cane like the one shown on the cake on the left, it must be 28g so that it will spiral easily.

GARDENER'S CAKE

Black-eyed Susan is trained up a bamboo cane to make an original cake for a keen gardener.

SOUTHERN AFRICA

There is nowhere in the world that I enjoy visiting more than Southern Africa. I am delighted that I have had so many opportunities to spend time in this beautiful and fascinating area. I always look forward to teaching there. Whenever I am in Southern Africa, I try to include at least one trip to the game reserves.

Even the currency of South Africa recognizes the importance of flowers with the protea being depicted on some coins and a group of native flowers on others. The coastal strip between Cape Town and Durban is known as the 'garden route' and contains the largest concentration of different flowers in the world. More than two thousand varieties can be seen there.

Steps have been taken to ensure that wild flowers do not become extinct by the creation of special reserves in some places. The wild flower show, held each spring at Caledon, south-east of Cape Town, has become a major tourist attraction.

Both South Africa and Zimbabwe have a very strong tradition of cake decorating. Filigree work and moulded flowers are particularly popular forms of sugarcraft.

The red dust and earth tones of the icing on the two-tier wedding cake represent the veldt. A pattern for making a template for the frieze of wild animals is given on page 144. The flame lilies, used to decorate the cake, grow in astonishing abundance in dry desolate areas of Zimbabwe. Their vibrant colours make a dramatic contrast to such a habitat. Considerable patience is required to reproduce the intricate flowers in sugar but they look superb.

UNITED KINGDOM

Many festive occasions are celebrated in the United Kingdom with a special cake . . . for instance, Christmas, Easter, St. Valentine's Day, christenings and birthdays, quite apart from weddings and anniversaries. Marzipan and royal icing are traditionally used to cover rich fruit cakes, but rolled fondant or sugarpaste is now quite frequently preferred for its greater versatility.

The large numbers of British people who emigrated to Australasia and South Africa earlier this century continued the traditional style of cake icing in their new homelands. Individual styles evolved over the years but sugarcraft is one culinary art form that owes much to the United Kingdom.

In the days before colour photographs became an essential feature of cookbooks, engravings were used to illustrate the elaborate designs favoured at the turn of the century. Tastes change in cake decorating as in everything else and there is now a trend towards more natural forms of decoration.

An ability to draw flowers accurately was much prized by the Victorians and Edwardians. Several books have been published recently containing their exquisite work which is a source of inspiration. The current awareness of conservation is reflected in the growing popularity of wild flowers as a theme in cake decorating. These are often used in the design of a cake for a wedding reception held in a country house or garden.

This cake was created for a farmer's daughter who was marrying at harvest-time. The field mice add a light-hearted touch to the two-tier cake. The red poppies look most effective combined with wheat.

WHEAT

Triticum

Wheat looks very effective when reproduced in flower paste. It gives height and lightness to an arrangement or spray. Many grasses and sedges can be made following the same basic principles. For reference, you could pick a few specimens of the numerous varieties that can be found on the roadside. You could also find inspiration in the exquisite drawings of the renowned Victorian botanist, the Reverend W. Keble Martin. Wheat has been used with poppies on the wedding cake shown on page 129.

EQUIPMENT

paste colours and dusting powders

stamen cotton

porcupine quill

covered wire

white florist's tape

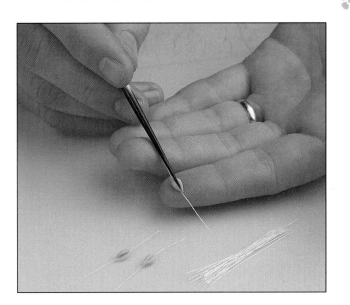

You may need to stiffen some stamen cotton with a sugar and water solution or starch as it needs to be quite firm.

Thread the cotton through a small piece of beige/yellow-coloured flower paste, leaving about 2.5cm (1in) at one end. Mould the paste into an oval and vein down the centre, as shown, using a porcupine quill or cocktail stick (toothpick). You will need to make about 20–25 seed heads for each ear of wheat. Leave to dry.

Tape three pieces of 26g wire together with white florist's tape. Then tape each seed head on to the wire, as shown, until the desired size of ear is achieved. Trim off the excess cotton with a pair of scissors and bend the remaining cotton for a natural effect, as shown.

Dust the seed heads with a mixture of yellow and brown dusting powders to give shading. Mix some white powder with clear spirit, then add some green and cream to match the colour of the stems. Use this to paint about 5–7.5cm (2–3in) of the tape-covered wires.

Roll out some more of the beige/yellow-coloured flower paste. Cut out some long pointed leaves. Mould these on to the stem, working down from the painted part to the base. When dry, paint the leaves with the same mixture used for the stems.

POPPY

Papaver Rhoeas

Although there are several varieties of poppies, both wild and cultivated, in different shades, the most familiar is certainly the bright red corn or field poppy. Such poppies can frequently be seen throughout the English countryside in the summer months, particularly in cornfields. An arrangement of poppies and wheat ears is an appropriate way of decorating a tiered cake for a country wedding, as shown on page 129. A spray of poppies including some seed heads also looks attractive on a birthday or other celebration cake.

EQUIPMENT

paste colours and dusting powder
former
calyx cutter
veining tool
ball tool
black stamens
porcupine quill
green-covered wire
green florist's tape
fine embroidery scissors
tweezers

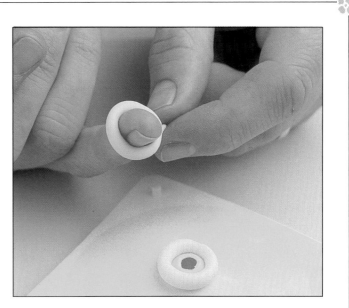

Roll some white flower paste into a sausage shape and wrap around your little finger, as shown. Pinch off the excess to make a ring. Place this on a former which has been lightly greased with vegetable fat.

Roll out some green-coloured flower paste and cut out a small calyx. Place this inside the white paste ring, as shown.

Roll out some red-coloured flower paste and cut out the two large petals. Vein and cup with a ball tool. Place over a former so that they keep their shape. Leave to dry for about 10 minutes so that the petals set slightly.

Vein and cup the two petals. Then position, as shown, in the calyx, sticking with egg white. Support the petals with pieces of foam rubber.

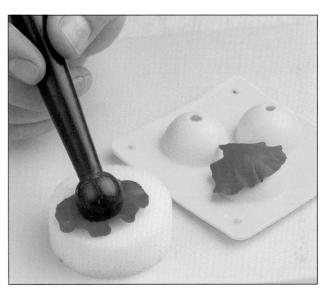

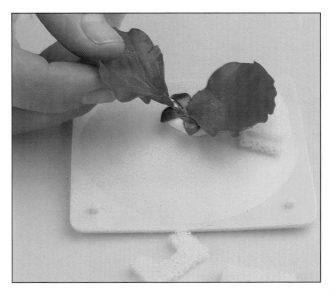

continued overleaf

POPPY
continued

Roll out some more red-coloured flower paste and cut out two smaller petals. Vein and cup. Place on the other petals, as shown, and support with pieces of foam rubber. Position a ring of black stamens, as shown.

Mould some green-coloured flower paste into a cone for the centre. Mark with a porcupine quill, as shown, and stick inside the ring of stamens with a little egg white. Leave to dry.

Dust the petals with red dusting powder to give some shading.

If you wish to wire the poppies, tape three pieces of 26g wire together. Place a calyx on the top of the wire. Leave to dry and then stick the petals into the calyx, using a little softened flower paste.

Make the buds from cones of green-coloured flower paste attached to pieces of thickened wire. Cut the small hairs with fine embroidery scissors. Mark the seed pods with a porcupine quill, then pinch with tweezers and cup with a ball tool.

Make some leaves in green-coloured flower paste. Either cut these out free-hand or use a fresh leaf as a template.

Tape an arrangement of poppies, leaves and seed pods together, as shown in the main photograph.

THISTLE

Onopordon acanthium

The thistle is the heraldic emblem of Scotland but it does grow all over the United Kingdom. As with most plants, there are many types, not necessarily all closely related botanically. If you cannot find a specimen growing nearby, it is best to refer to a book on wild flowers for the exact shape and size. The top part of the thistle shown here has been made with cotton, as this gives the most realistic result, but a similar effect could be achieved by piping royal icing on to a small piece of flower paste.

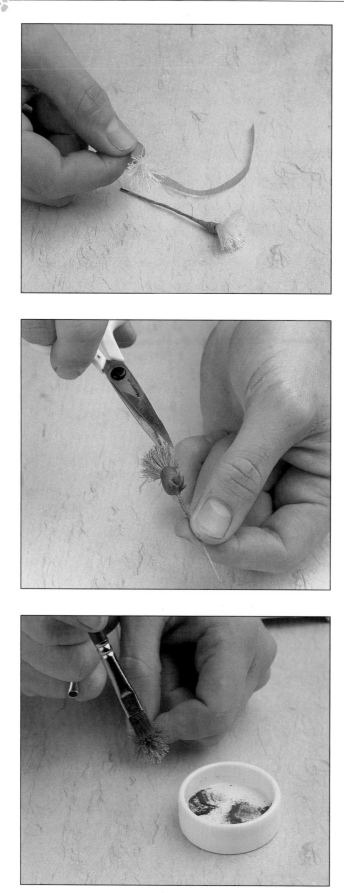

THISTLE

EQUIPMENT

paste colours and dusting powders
ivory cotton
green-covered wires
green florist's tape
flat paintbrush
fine embroidery scissors

Wind some ivory cotton round your index finger from 80–100 times, depending on how full you want the thistle head to be. Wrap a piece of 30g wire tightly around the base of the hank of cotton.

Tape a piece of 26g wire to the piece of 30g wire with green florist's tape. Trim off the excess cotton to make the thistle head as shown. Use a flat paintbrush to dust a mixture of plum and violet dusting powders on the cotton to give it the required shading.

Roll a small ball of green-coloured flower paste. Thread this up the wire, sticking around the thistle head with egg white. Using fine embroidery scissors, cut the base as shown, starting from the bottom and working up.

A real leaf was used as a template for the leaves made in green-coloured flower paste. Dust the backs of the leaves with white dusting powder. Leave to dry and then brush vegetable fat over the leaves to give a natural gloss.

THISTLE CAKE

The thistle is an appropriate emblem for this cake designed for a Hogmanay party. The tartan ribbon emphasizes the Scottish theme.

HAZEL

Coryllus

Several trees including the hazel have hanging inflorescences or pendulous spikes, commonly known as catkins. These appear before the tree bursts into leaf in the spring. They are very quick to make in sugar and are an attractive background for spring flowers such as the daffodils shown on the cake on page 142. Pussy willow can be made in a similar way. You can make the catkins as large or small as you like depending on the size and scale of the other flowers used.

EQUIPMENT

paste colours and dusting powders

brown florist's tape

covered wire

brown cotton (thread)

semolina, ground rice or maize meal

tweezers

Cut some brown florist's tape into ⅓- or ¼-widths. Cover several strands of 30g or 33g wire, then cut into shorter pieces. Tape together, as shown, to make little branches. Make sure that they are taped together tightly to give a good finish. Tape several of these branches on to a cocktail stick (toothpick) or a piece of satay stick.

Squash a pea-sized piece of green-coloured flower paste. Place a piece of brown cotton (thread) in the centre and mould the paste into a ball again, thus securing the cotton. Roll into a tapered sausage shape, as shown.

Brush with egg white and then roll in yellow-coloured semolina, ground rice or maize meal to represent the pollen, as shown. Shake off the excess.

Use tweezers to tie the catkins on to the branches, making sure that the knots are tight. This demands some patience as it is quite fiddly.

When all the catkins are in position, mix some white dusting powder with clear spirit. Add some brown paste colour to the mixture and paint all over the branches to give a natural effect. Before this dries, dust some green dusting powder in small areas over the branches.

When the catkins are dry, dust a little green dusting powder lightly down one side of each.

DAFFODIL

Narcissus

Immortalized in Wordsworth's poem, daffodils are always associated with springtime in England, although they also grow in many other parts of the world. There are hundreds of different varieties, so the flowering season extends over several weeks. The daffodil is the national flower of Wales and some Welsh people wear them as buttonholes on St. David's day. A small rockery alpine daffodil is shown here but other varieties can be made in the same way. The flowers look most natural when they stand upright as arranged on the cake overleaf.

EQUIPMENT

paste colours and dusting powders
daffodil cutters
sweetcorn (mealie) leaf veiner
green-covered wire
ball tool
piping nozzle (tip)
small yellow stamens
semolina, ground rice or maize meal

Mould a ball of yellow-coloured flower paste into a Mexican hat shape. Then roll from the inside outwards until it is large enough to cut out the back petal shape. Place the cutter over the cone to cut this out. Vein on a sweetcorn (mealie) leaf veiner on both sides, then mark the centre vein.

Dip a piece of hooked 26g wire in egg white and thread down through the throat. Mould around securely. Tape two further pieces of 26g wire to the original wire. Make a cavity with a ball tool.

Roll out some more paste thinly and cut out a petal. Vein both sides and the centre as before, then stick in position, as shown. Make a hole in the centre with a cocktail stick (toothpick). Pinch the petals to a slight point.

Roll out some orange-coloured flower paste and cut out the throat with a throat cutter. Frill the lower edge and mark ridges down it, as shown. Stick together to make the trumpet and place on a piping nozzle (tip) to dry.

Fold three small yellow stamens in half. Pull one up slightly and then tape them together, making five of the same size and one slightly longer. Brush with egg white and dip in yellow-coloured semolina, ground rice or maize meal to give the effect of pollen. Cut off the excess stamen cotton, leaving a small amount at the back. Stick this into the hole made with the cocktail stick. Place the trumpet in position, sticking down with egg white.

Bend the daffodil at the angle shown in the main photograph. Roll out some rust-coloured flower paste and cut out a pennant shape. Vein down the centre and place on the back of the flower. Leave to dry.

Dust all over with yellow dusting powder, then dust some green dusting powder on the tips of the petals, around the base of the flower and in the centre.

DAFFODIL CAKE

An arrangement of daffodils and catkins decorates this oval cake, cut at an angle to
give an impression of *art nouveau*.

PATTERNS FOR TEMPLATES

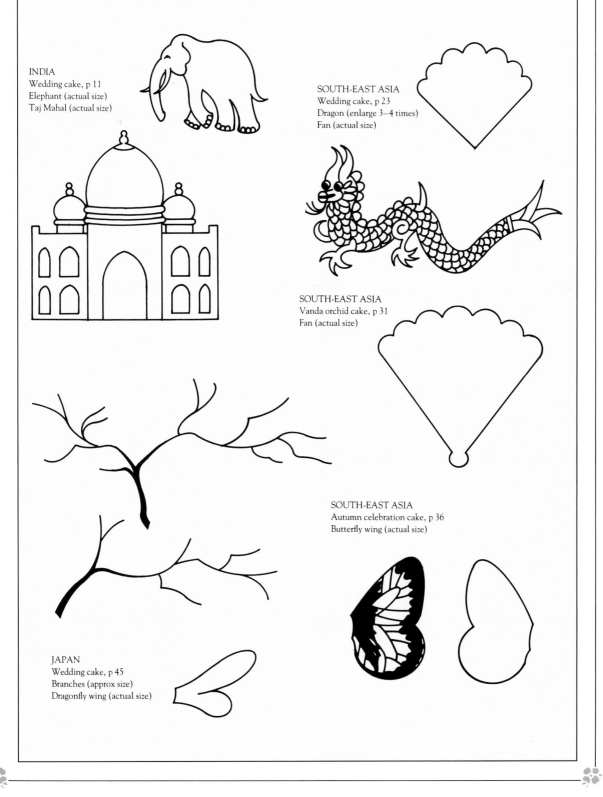

INDIA
Wedding cake, p 11
Elephant (actual size)
Taj Mahal (actual size)

SOUTH-EAST ASIA
Wedding cake, p 23
Dragon (enlarge 3–4 times)
Fan (actual size)

SOUTH-EAST ASIA
Vanda orchid cake, p 31
Fan (actual size)

SOUTH-EAST ASIA
Autumn celebration cake, p 36
Butterfly wing (actual size)

JAPAN
Wedding cake, p 45
Branches (approx size)
Dragonfly wing (actual size)

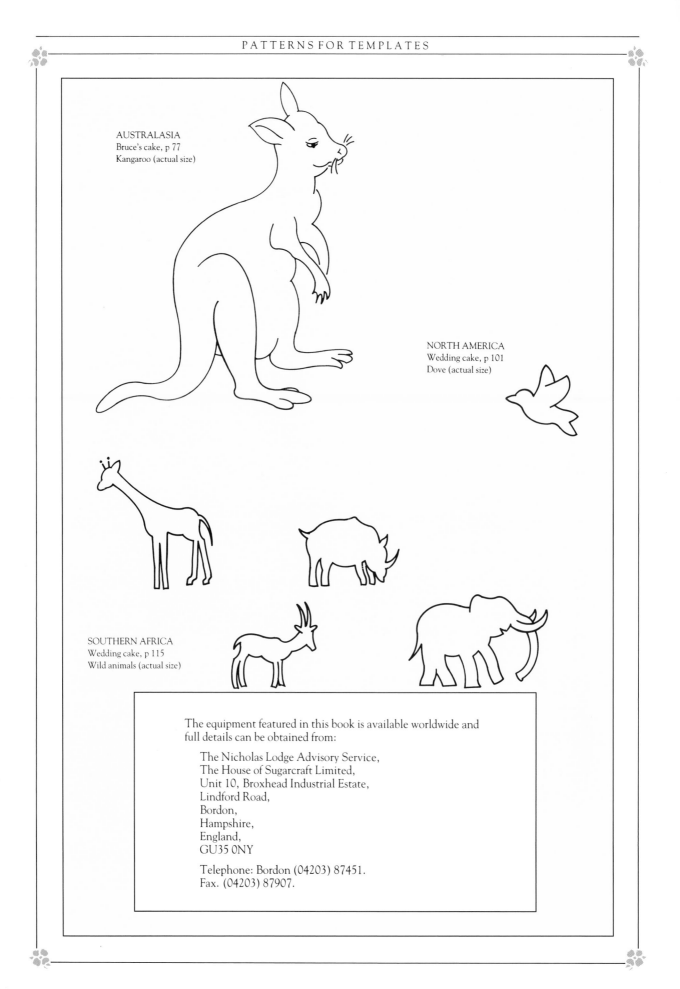

AUSTRALASIA
Bruce's cake, p 77
Kangaroo (actual size)

NORTH AMERICA
Wedding cake, p 101
Dove (actual size)

SOUTHERN AFRICA
Wedding cake, p 115
Wild animals (actual size)

The equipment featured in this book is available worldwide and full details can be obtained from:

The Nicholas Lodge Advisory Service,
The House of Sugarcraft Limited,
Unit 10, Broxhead Industrial Estate,
Lindford Road,
Bordon,
Hampshire,
England,
GU35 0NY

Telephone: Bordon (04203) 87451.
Fax. (04203) 87907.